GOOD
REASONABLE
PEOPLE

GOOD
REASONABLE
PEOPLE

THE PSYCHOLOGY BEHIND
AMERICA'S DANGEROUS DIVIDE

Keith Payne

VIKING

VIKING
An imprint of Penguin Random House LLC
penguinrandomhouse.com

LIBRARY OF CONGRESS CATALOGING-IN-PUBLICATION DATA

Names: Payne, Keith (Social scientist), author.
Title: Good reasonable people : the psychology behind
America's dangerous divide / Keith Payne.
Description: New York : Viking, [2024] | Includes
bibliographical references and index. |
Identifiers: LCCN 2024016424 (print) |
LCCN 2024016425 (ebook) | ISBN 9780593491942
(hardcover) | ISBN 9780593491959 (ebook)
Subjects: LCSH: Polarization (Social sciences)—United
States. | Social conflict—United States. |
Political culture—United States.
Classification: LCC HN90.P57 P39 2024 (print) |
LCC HN90.P57 (ebook) |
DDC 306.0973—dc23/eng/20240624
LC record available at https://lccn.loc.gov/2024016424
LC ebook record available at https://lccn.loc.gov/2024016425

Printed in the United States of America
1st Printing

Designed by Amanda Dewey

For my family,
who showed me that love and difference
are not enemies

CONTENTS

INTRODUCTION

I think there's just one kind of folks. Folks.

—SCOUT, in Harper Lee's
To Kill a Mockingbird

I should have kept scrolling. But we were four weeks into quarantine, and I'd had enough. Enough boredom, enough uncertainty, enough of my couch. I was staring out at the world through little screens that brought increasingly dire news about the pandemic raging across the world. I thought the pandemic would help bring Americans closer together, the way that in the movies alien invaders cause all humankind to band together against a common enemy. But in this virus, we were facing the biggest alien threat of our lifetimes, and people were already making it a topic of partisan bickering and finger-pointing.

In the middle of all this, my brother Brad was posting on that little screen about how President Trump had done "great things for this country" and how the fake news wouldn't give him a break. I normally refuse to get into political arguments on social media, but something in me let loose. I poured out a stream of comments about how Trump was not only incompetent but also immoral, and it was so plain to see that there was no need for fake news to call out the obvious. Brad responded that I couldn't handle being told I'm wrong, and I was in no position to talk about morality anyhow, seeing as I was an atheist. It went downhill from there.

Brad and I are just four years apart, the fourth- and fifth-born of seven brothers and sisters. But we are far apart in our views of how the world works. I'm a secular liberal college professor, living in a liberal college town a long way from where we grew up in western Kentucky. When Brad finished high school, he went to work as an electrician. He now lives in the mountains of Tennessee, where he attends an evangelical church. He's funny, irreverent, and all the brash parts of our father that I'm not.

I often felt that I was the strange one in the family. Things started changing as soon as I left for college. A few days before, my dad, Mitch, said, "Don't go off and turn into a goddamned long-haired hippie."

I said, "It's the nineties, Dad, and there haven't been any hippies for thirty years."

"I mean it," he said. "Don't you come back here with long hair and earrings." He had been watching TV when a rerun of *Little House on the Prairie*, with the actor Michael Landon, came on the screen. For some reason, Michael Landon always pissed him off. "Goddamned long-haired hippies," he said again, to no one in particular.

Not long after, I packed everything I owned—a newly bought rug rolled up in the back seat, my beat-up guitar, and a new suitcase full of old clothes. The suitcase was a graduation present. No one in my family owned luggage, because we didn't travel. I put it all in my Monte Carlo, the one that I had spent the previous summer sanding down to metal. Then I built it back up, layer after layer of primer and putty and sanding, until it was half car and half sculpture. My brother Jason painted it jet-black and tinted the windows. I drove, fast, to Lexington, three hours and a lifetime away.

It was Thanksgiving break when my tires pulled back into the gravel driveway. My hair was three months longer, and I had small hoop earrings. Two in each ear. I took a deep breath before I opened the door. Dad was sitting at his regular spot, the kitchen chair at the head of the table. From his perch he could see everything happening in the kitchen as well as the living room and the front door. His face lit up. "Hey! There he is!" he boomed. He welcomed me in with a hug and pretended not to notice a thing. He never mentioned the hair or the earrings. That's typical of my family. We argue, mock each other, and occasionally tell each other to go to hell. But we don't have the heart to follow through.

So many families like mine have reached a brittle peace in recent years, holding their tongues and holding their breath, limiting their conversations to the weather and sports and children. Or worse, they have not found any peace at all. I recently encountered a genre of online videos in which young adults tearfully disown their parents, explaining why their values are simply too immoral to continue contact. It's a strange reversal from the scenes played out when I was in college, when some of my friends came out to their parents as gay and achingly waited to see if they would be embraced or rejected. Now, the young are passing judgment on the old, and partisanship has invaded every aspect of life.

Most Democratic singles refuse to date Trump supporters. Politics is increasingly defining who is "our" kind of people and who is not. I expect all families, particularly large ones, by now have felt the consternation that comes when two people look at the same thing in broad daylight and cannot agree on what they are looking at. Exasperated, we wonder how they can believe what they are saying.

I remember listening to Rush Limbaugh on my drive to high school in the morning and thinking it was funny. I would pull out of our driveway onto the two-lane blacktop of Highway 60. After a mile, I'd pass the truck stop where I used to buy candy and hang out before I was old enough to drive. Farther on, I'd pass the Catholic church and elementary school I had attended; across the road from it was a juvenile detention center surrounded by gleaming barbed wire. We joked that it was conveniently located, so there was no need for a pipeline from school to prison.

A couple more miles and I would pass the distillery that made Kentucky Tavern, Dad's favorite bourbon and an all-purpose medication for toothaches, sore gums, and insomnia. Then there was the steel mill where my uncle worked for most of his life. At night you could see the orange glow from the furnaces inside. I once asked him if it was hot in there. He looked at me for a moment with weary eyes, as if he was trying to figure out if I was being a wiseass or not. Then he just said, "Yes, buddy. It gets awful hot." Past that was the power plant, where my brother Jason would later work, its two giant stacks billowing coal smoke day and night.

Driving through this landscape, I listened to Limbaugh make fun of welfare moochers who sponged off hardworking Americans. It never occurred to me to doubt that we were the hardworking Americans, despite the free lunches I received, the food stamps Mom spent, and the tinfoil-wrapped boxes of government cheese that arrived at our doorstep. It was fun to laugh with Limbaugh at feminists, especially since I didn't know any feminists. What I knew was that the Bible instructed women to submit to their husbands as to the Lord. My mother reminded me of it often. It was easy to nod along with Rush Limbaugh's generalizations about Black people, since I didn't know any Black people. My hometown of Maceo was then, as now, 100 percent White. I often heard the phrase "that's mighty white of you" as a synonym for "thank you." Friends used the N-word furtively, with the illicit thrill of an eight-year-old saying "fuck."

All these years later it's not difficult for me to flip back to that mindset, if I want to. There's a simplicity to it, as if the world switched from a Picasso to a Vermeer painting. There's a certainty about right and wrong that comes from feeling you have God on your side. There's a lightness that comes from being sure that the world is fair: if you work hard, you'll be fine. I can't stay there for long though. I've learned too much about history and science, and about the consequences of inequality and discrimination. Still, visiting that mindset from time to time helps humanize people who disagree with me.

We need more humanizing, because people in our country have been dehumanizing one another a lot. Democrats call Trump supporters MAGAts. Republicans call Democrats demon rats. And countless angry social media posts call one another scum, slime, or worse. Psychologists recently gave a nationally representative sample of research participants an "ascent of man" type image. On the left was a hunched, apelike silhouette. Then each successive figure stands up straighter, until on the right it is a silhouette of a human. The participants were asked to select the image that best represents how evolved Republicans and Democrats are. The more closely attached people were to their own party, the more they depicted the other party as apelike.

It's not just name-calling. Decades of research have found that dehumanizing words and images are a strong predictor that political violence is around the corner. The Nazis famously depicted Jews as rats. In the Rwandan genocide, Hutus called Tutsis cockroaches. And Black Americans were depicted as apes in the Jim Crow South. Dehumanizing other people places them outside the circle of moral concern and makes violence much easier.

Scholars who study political violence around the world say that all the risk factors are in place, and the warning lights are flashing red. One of them is commonly using dehumanizing language about the other side. A second warning sign is when political differences align with racial or religious group differences. And a third is a history of political violence. Uh-oh.

We have a history of extraordinary political violence, from the Civil War, to lynchings, to assassinations. Attempts have been made on the lives of one in three U.S. presidents. Our political divisions are aligned more and more with racial and religious divisions. Racially motivated hate crimes have almost doubled since 2014, according to the FBI. Surveys in 2018 found that around 15 percent of Americans felt it was justified for their party to use violence, double the rate of just a few years earlier. That figure is even higher if the other side provokes them first. Of course, we always view the other side as provoking us first. We are caught in a classic cycle of escalation that could easily spiral out of control.

The stakes are high, but what happens depends largely on choices we make and how we understand one another. The aim of this book is to understand the sources and consequences of our political divisions from a psychological perspective. We have entered an era of extreme views and radical behavior, at least among some segments of society. The immediate future is full of peril for American democracy. And yet, the psychology behind this tumult is the same that drove our choices during much more peaceful decades. In fact, the basic facts of human psychology have not changed in tens of thousands of years. We are working with the same cognitive hardware that elevated kings and queens and then beheaded them. It's the same hardware that wrote the Declaration of Independence and the Constitution, then several decades later wrote articles of secession. Ordinary principles of psychology can lead to extraordinary actions when they run up against exceptional moments in history. One such moment has arrived.

A lot of writing has analyzed what polarization means for electoral horse races. Because the country is evenly divided, news stories and essays tend to focus on events and ideas that might tip a close election. That means they focus on factors like inflation, gas prices, how well the economy is doing, candidate messaging, and how much candidates have spent on political advertising. The intense news coverage creates the false impression that those are factors that drive politics for most people. In reality, those factors might only shift ten or twenty thousand votes. They are important for election outcomes, but in a country that is divided nearly fifty-fifty, every tiny factor that influences 1 or 2 percent of the votes matters for election outcomes. Elections are obviously important, but the factors that swing close elections are not the factors that explain why the vast majority of people vote the way they do or believe the things they believe. This book is about why we are evenly divided in the first place, and that has little to do with how the economy is doing or political ads.

Plenty of essays and books have delved into the differences between progressivism and liberalism. Or neoconservatism and traditional conservatism. Or why traditional conservatism is really classical liberalism. All of the isms turn political and social life into a complex web of ideologies that might be important for academics and journalists but don't mean much for the average person. Abstract ideas like socialism, racism, or fascism have become a primary way scholars go about understanding politics, and I think that's a shame. The problem is that isms take interesting things that human beings do and turn them into abstractions with fuzzy boundaries. Then, when we want to talk about people doing interesting things, we have to argue that this particular thing is an instance of the general abstraction. Is this policy a case of socialism? Is that decision an instance of racism?

Throughout the book, I try to avoid using abstract isms. My goal is more personal. I want to focus on what our divisions mean for us as individuals, as families, and as communities. Whenever I encounter an ism, I want to take it apart and ask what people are actually doing, why they do it, and what it means to them. This book is not about politicians or political strategists or party organizations. It is about ordinary people making sense of their world in the best way they know how.

Sometimes it is shocking how differently people make sense of the same world. It has become more and more apparent for many of us in recent years that other people we thought we knew don't just disagree with us; they see the world in a deeply different way than we do. The question is: Why? In this book I try to answer that question by understanding how people think about politics, the deeper meanings and identities behind our political worldviews, and why talking about it is so hard.

Most psychological accounts of the differences between liberals and conservatives focus on personality traits. They produce explanations in the form of "Liberals are like this, but conservatives are like that." One popular theory argues that liberals, but not conservatives, are high on a personality trait called openness to experience.

People who are open to experience like to try new and different things. They like to travel, to eat strange new foods from cultures around the world, and to listen to kinds of music they've never heard before. They like to do all the things that people low in openness to experience call weird. People who are low on the trait have more conventional tastes. They like traditional food, art, and entertainment. They like to do things they consider normal. It is easy to see how being open to experience fits our stereotyped mental images of cosmopolitan, epicurean liberals, while being less open fits our images of buttoned-up conservatives. According to this theory, the liberal mind is a playful mind, and the conservative mind is a cautious mind.

One version of the openness theory argues that these personality differences are rooted in biological differences in sensitivity to threats. Studies show, for example, that conservatives are more revolted than liberals by the sight or smell of disgusting things. They also may have a stronger biological fear response to threats. Everyone shows an involuntary startle response when a sudden loud noise rings out, but conservatives jump a little higher than liberals do. Emotions like disgust and fear have evolved to protect us from threats. Disgust motivates us to avoid rotten food, excrement, and other things that might carry infectious disease. Fear prompts us to avoid physical threats to our safety. But we rely on emotions to manage not only physical threats but also social ones. This emotion-based theory says that the reason liberals are more open to new experiences is because they are less emotionally sensitive to threats. Or stated differently, people who have highly sensitive emotional reactions to threats will be attracted to conservative ideas as a way to manage threats.

Another popular theory argues that liberals are flexible thinkers, while conservatives are cognitively rigid. Studies show that conservatives score higher on a trait called need for structure, and another called need for closure. The idea is that conservatives want neat and simple answers, whereas liberals are comfortable with the messy gray areas of life. Other studies have found that liberals perform better on cognitive tests that require changing your frame of thinking. Conservatives perform better on cognitive tests that require sticking to a script and doing the same thing over and over. These findings are often interpreted as being flattering to liberals (freethinkers!) and unflattering to conservatives (dogmatic!), but they can just as easily be interpreted as saying that conservatives stick to principles and think decisively, whereas liberals are wishy-washy. According to this theory, the liberal mind is limber, but the conservative mind is unbending.

The most popular theory for explaining ideological differences is the Moral Foundations Theory, which argues that liberals and conservatives have fundamentally different moral values. Both conservatives and liberals care about avoiding harm and being fair, but that is about all they share. Conservatives care much more than liberals about other values, such as loyalty to one's group, moral purity (that is, protecting the sacred), and authority (that is, respect and obedience to social hierarchies). These foundations are described as modules, like little switches in the mind that turn on or off to trigger different mental reactions.

These theories all capture something real about the psychology behind politics. Lots of research shows that liberals really do score a few percentage points higher on openness to experience than conservatives. People's political orientation is correlated with their thinking styles and emotional reactions. And conservatives do report valuing purity, authority, and loyalty somewhat more than liberals do (about 1 point more on a 6-point scale). But ultimately, I believe these theories are not very helpful in explaining why we see the world differently, for two reasons.

First, the differences are tiny. Personality traits, thinking styles, and values can explain only a few percentage points of the differences between partisans. They are just not large enough to explain the giant gulf separating us.

Second, and even more fundamental, these theories don't tell us what we really want to know. They *describe* some of the differences between partisans, but as we will see in the chapters ahead, they are limited in their ability to *explain how and why* our political divides have come to take the shape they have. The sentence "Opium induces sleep because it is a soporific" is a classic example used in teaching the logical fallacy of circular reasoning. At first glance, it seems to explain something. But "soporific" just means "sleep-inducing." So the sentence doesn't really explain anything; it just relabels it. The same thing happens with explanations based on isms, or those based on some inner property of the person. What makes these theories appealing is that they promise, at first glance, to give us insight into the ways that conservatives are essentially different from liberals. They play into the human desire to explain events by appealing to an inner essence that makes them what they are.

Essentialism is appealing because it is simple. Children come to understand the world by essentializing, because it helps track features that regularly go together. But it leads to errors. Preschoolers, for example, predict that a baby switched at birth will speak the language of its biological parents, not the parents who raise it, because of the kind of baby it "really" is. If asked, they think caterpillars have a different kind of blood than spiders do, because a caterpillar seems like a very different kind of thing than a spider. Tomatoes, young children will insist, have juicy vitamins, but carrots have solid vitamins.

Our tendency to focus on inner essences even extends to objects associated with people. We value a Picasso painting much more than an exact copy because it is the real thing. People will pay a lot of money for gum that was chewed by Britney Spears, or a sweater once worn by Marilyn Monroe, because it was connected in some way to the real people. But most won't buy a sweater once worn by Hitler. They won't even try it on. Evil and goodness are not contagious infections, and a sweater is nothing but woven threads. But it seems to carry with it some traces of the inner essence of the owner, transferred by touch as if it were some magic talisman.

If someone disagrees with us, the easiest way to explain it is by appealing to something about the inner qualities of the person. We often assume that they must be ignorant, unintelligent, or arguing in bad faith, because deep down, anyone can see the truth as we do if they have the right facts. Modern psychology theories are a bit more sophisticated than that. They don't usually assume ignorance or unintelligence, but they often assume underlying personality traits or values that make some people like this but other people like that. By essentializing, we hope to gain a glimpse of the liberal mind and the conservative mind at work. But to me, essentializing theories ultimately leave us disappointed, because *there is no liberal mind or conservative mind*. There are only human minds trying to make sense of the circumstances in which they find themselves.

Personality differences have a hard time explaining the biggest predictors of partisanship. For example, about 90 percent of Black Americans and two thirds of Hispanic Americans support Democrats. About 60 percent of Whites support Republicans, and the

Republican Party is more than 80 percent White. The likelihood that differences that large would happen by chance is impossibly small. In the social sciences, it is exceedingly rare to be able to account for 80 or 90 percent of any aspect of human behavior with a single variable, because human behavior is so complex. Any theory of political identities that does not grapple with these enormous differences is ignoring the elephant (or donkey?) in the room.

Are Black and Hispanic people really that much more open to experience than White people? Do they think so much more flexibly? And how in the world did innate modules for valuing social hierarchies end up primarily in the minds of White people? These personality-based theories don't do a very good job of explaining why our politics is so fractured around social groups.

The same problem holds for other sources of division. Why do about two thirds of people with an advanced degree support Democrats, whereas a similar majority of high school graduates support Republicans? Why did more than 80 percent of evangelical Christians support Donald Trump in 2020, while two thirds of the nonreligious voted for Joe Biden? The few percentage points that separate Democrats and Republicans on personality traits or values can't come close to accounting for the chasms between the educated and the less educated, or evangelicals and the nonreligious.

The circumstances that push us in one political direction or the other are not only demographic. As we will see, the history of the particular city or town where people live casts a long shadow. We can predict the political leanings of residents today based on the systems of racial segregation and inequality that were set up decades ago. And we can predict with chilling accuracy where those systems were built by knowing how many people were enslaved in that city or town on the eve of the Civil War.

Arguments over history and race have become a political flash-point. But they are often framed around whether the United States is "fundamentally racist." This is just another version of essentialism, which is as misguided when talking about a country as when talking about individuals. A country isn't "fundamentally" racist or not. There is no inner essence that makes a country what it is. Instead, there is a complex web of causes and effects. Our job, as I see it, is to understand how the facts and choices of the past have led to the circumstances in which we find ourselves today.

As a social psychologist, I study the ways that people respond to their social circumstances. My research suggests that our political tribes are primarily the result not of our inner essences but of our circumstances. Our political divisions result from basic facts about how all human minds work, when those minds find themselves in different situations. These circumstances, partly chosen and partly beyond our control, set us on very different paths. Once we start down those paths, we bend our view of the world to make sense from where we are standing.

My task in this book is to try to explain how people make sense of the world from these different circumstances, and therefore why the world looks so different from their various points of view. So we need to understand the history that has led us to our present circumstance, and the ways that the human mind goes about sensemaking. The degree of conflict and animosity around politics really has become much worse over the last two decades. But the people haven't changed. Our minds haven't changed. What has changed, as I argue in the final chapter, is our political environment.

To many people, the idea that liberals and conservatives differ not in our minds but in our circumstances feels unsatisfying.

When we get into arguments with people on the other side, they certainly seem deeply different. When I give talks about my research, audience members will often come up to me afterward and tell me about a relative or a high school friend on the other side who is so irrational that there must be something deeply wrong with them. I think the simpler explanation is that there is something in all of us that desires—maybe even needs—to see *them* as utterly alien from *us*. Because if we are not essentially different, and our differences follow from the hands we are given to play in life, then that means that you or I could easily have been on the other side if things had shaken out a little differently. That is an uncomfortable thought for many people. Although this book is about the psychology of our political divisions, it is not about what is wrong with the other side. It is about understanding our own minds, our own circumstances, and our own blind spots as much as understanding those of other people.

In the chapters that follow I will explore how history, race, class, religion, and urban versus rural living set us on different paths, and how we come to rationalize our own point of view as the only right point of view. We will see how the same psychological responses that sort us into partisan groups attract us to a range of other ideas we fight about, from what counts as "fake news" to conspiracy theories. Those very same psychological responses blind us to our own logical contradictions. And they make it hard to have civil conversations about any of it, because we see our own side as arguing in good faith, but we see the other side as intentionally trying to do harm.

Understanding the psychology behind our political divide provides clues about how we can reduce the damage it is causing. To be clear, the message of this book is not a mushy "let's all just get along." There are good reasons for today's partisan divides. I believe that some ideas are better than others, and that those ideas are worth fighting for. But the beautiful thing about the fragile experiment we call democracy is that it allows us to fight with words and votes, not guns and blood. Understanding the roots of our division can give us the tools to stop going around in circles in frustrating arguments. It can help us make better choices about how we engage in political debates, how policymakers and social media companies deal with misinformation, and how we deal with one another on social media. It can help us separate, if we choose to, our political principles from our personal relationships, so that we can nurture both.

This book is part science, part history, and part memoir. The only way I know to tell this story is the way I learned it myself. So I'd like to introduce you to some places and people you ought to know.

GOOD
REASONABLE
PEOPLE

ONE

THE ROOTS OF OUR DIVISION
Time, Place, History

The past is never dead. It's not even past.

—WILLIAM FAULKNER

alf an hour's drive outside Lexington, Kentucky, you'll pass a sprawling castle. It's an honest-to-God castle made of stone, with turrets and a wall. The castle is in a town called Versailles. It's pronounced "ver-*sails*." If you try to pronounce it like the place Marie Antoinette lived, you will immediately be dismissed as an ignoramus and, worse, an outsider.

The landscape in that part of Kentucky looks like the post-cards. There are rolling green hills with miles of white fences that let you know you are in horse country. This is the part of the state that has money. Nearby, in Bardstown, they distill bourbon. They run the Derby next door in Louisville. And all over the state, they raise tobacco. A place built on whiskey, smoking, and gambling is bound to have some colorful characters. But I want to show you that this place also holds clues to understanding our divided cultural moment, when cleavages of politics, race, class, and religion are making us rethink the world we once understood, and making us reconsider the people we thought we knew.

East of Lexington, the hills twist and yaw into the Appalachian Mountains. The Appalachians are so ancient that they formed when North America and Africa were still moving toward each other. It was before the dinosaurs, when plants ruled the earth and the best the animal kingdom had come up with were insects and scorpions. The continents plowed slowly into each other, pushing up the Appalachians like the wrinkle of metal when two cars collide. The highways in that part of the country cut straight through mountains, where sheer faces in the rock on both sides of the road were cut by explosives. You can still see the vertical lines in the rock where men drilled holes and dropped sticks of dynamite to send the sides of mountains tumbling down. In the middle of those rock faces, little streams of water pour out. There's no hole, no tunnel. It just streams through the rock itself. In the winter they form slow-motion waterfalls of ice. To the people who live there, the mountains define their world. Towns exist only in the valleys between them, and they are not like in other parts of the country, where towns are square grids of streets. Here, a town is a single winding road at the bottom of the valley, with a line of weathered buildings on either side. From the air they look like dirty ribbons a child left behind.

But I did not grow up in the mountains. I grew up on the other side of Lexington, as the hills give way to the flat ground of western Kentucky. The landscape looked more like the plains and farmland of Illinois than the mountains to the east. A drive through that country is a flickering reel of corn, tobacco, and soybean fields. Here and there, a red tobacco barn. A curious number of the trees along the highway are slumped, even in summer, from the winter ice storms. The ice thaws quickly but leaves its marks long after on the trees' hunched backs.

Our house was one of thirteen houses along Highway 60 in Maceo, population 400. The speed limit was 55, but it was a straight shot through the country, so the cars and eighteen-wheelers barreled through much faster. One summer day my brothers and I were playing in the front yard when a car ran off the road. As its right two tires left the road they sunk into the small drainage ditch separating our yard from the highway. The car flipped over and dug a trail through our yard, coming to rest upside down, halfway into the neighbor's driveway. I didn't see anything after that because my brothers and I were shooed inside. When we asked what happened to the people in the car, Mom said they would be fine and then changed the subject. We were not allowed to watch at the windows, so I could only see the blue and red lights flashing on the walls of the living room.

Highway 60 was a critical part of our lives, an artery connecting us to everything else. People who grow up in a town or a subdivision are not so dependent on a single piece of road, because their streets connect to other streets a block away. If one road is blocked, they can easily take another. But out in the country, if the highway was closed for some reason, we had to drive a half hour or more out of the way to get where we were going via the back roads. I knew our stretch of blacktop in minute detail, like the place where the white lines went wavy because the truck that was painting them swerved to avoid hitting a dog.

It was the road we took "into town" each day for school or church or the grocery. Going into town meant driving twenty minutes into Owensboro, a city with a population of about sixty thousand today. Almost every trip took us toward Owensboro, until sometime in the 1980s, when Mom stopped attending the Catholic church that we had always gone to. She started going to a Baptist church that was in the other direction, farther away from town. That was the start of a lot of conflict in my family, as Dad had not converted with her. We didn't know it at the time, but the schism we were experiencing in my family was part of a trend happening all over the country. Some Protestant denominations were becoming aligned with conservative politics in a way that had not happened before. Now Christians who were called "born again," "fundamentalist," or "evangelical" were pulling away from mainline Protestant and Catholic churches. Mom didn't like those labels. Her favorite was "Pentecostal," named after the time the Holy Spirit appeared as tongues of fire above the heads of the disciples to distinguish the true believers from the infidels. My parents started to argue about what religion the children would be brought up in. Their arguments got angrier than they had ever been before, because now they had the edge of God's Truth, and the stakes were eternal hellfire.

Still, the highway was our only connection to the rest of the world. My siblings and I would ride our bikes along the shoulder to the truck stop a mile away. We could buy candy at the gas station. Sometimes my parents would send me to pick up a pack of cigarettes. I was nervous the first time, thinking that the clerk wouldn't believe me that they were for my parents and I would be in trouble. But she just put the Winstons down on the counter next to the red hot jawbreakers without asking any questions. Sometimes we would buy french fries and cokes at the diner and pretend we were in a city where you could just leave your house and walk into a restaurant. The waitress called us honey. The truckers ignored us.

And in the parking lot you could find treasures, like plastic cigarette lighters and discarded issues of *Playboy*.

My parents, Mitch and Paula, bought the house on Highway 60 for $30,000 on a thirty-year mortgage, now long paid off. It has white aluminum siding, three bedrooms, and one bathroom. They raised seven of us in that house. My oldest brother, Jason, moved out on his own while I was still a baby. The next two oldest were my sisters, Shannon and Vicki. They shared one of the bedrooms. I shared the boys' room with my younger brothers, Brad, Eric, and Mark.

My most vivid memories of that house are from the perspective of a child, looking up from the floor. I remember the baseboards and the electrical outlets in detail, and the bottoms of the gold-colored drapes that covered the picture window looking out onto the highway. I remember the thick loops of the brown shag carpet in the living room, where I would sit to play or watch TV. We had a big television, with the screen enclosed in a faux wooden case. One day it stopped working, so Dad came home with a smaller one that he stacked on top of it. It stayed like that for years. My sister asked when he was going to get rid of the bottom one, because it looked tacky. Dad said, look how lucky we are, we have two TV sets when some people don't have any.

To relieve the tight space, Dad added on a room. He built it from the carport, a slab of concrete on one end of the house that the roof extended over. Dad and some of his friends framed the walls and floor themselves. They put up wood-grain paneling on the walls and linoleum on the floor. It was the biggest room in the house. And yet, it never felt like a part of the house. Instead of furnishing it with a couch or some chairs like a living room, Dad hung a porch swing from the ceiling. He installed a wood-burning stove to save on heating bills in the winter. That meant there was always a pile of split wood in the room, and just outside the door in the yard was a pile of logs waiting to be split. In the spring it was a hothouse for tomato plants waiting to be set out in the garden. In the summer it was a greenhouse where hundreds of tomatoes sat ripening. And in the winter, it was a cellar storing musty-smelling potatoes. Somehow that room always felt half finished and half outdoors. To this day, we call it the carport.

I can't think about the house I grew up in without thinking about that room. It's the physical embodiment of the way we lived. The house itself was small but tidy. Mom was constantly cooking and cleaning up after her brood, never caught up but never entirely overwhelmed either. The front yard had flower beds with neat borders that Mom tended with care. We had one hand groping toward the middle class. But chaos was always one step away.

A few years ago I sat visiting at the kitchen table with Mom and Dad, now a clean table in a quiet house. "It's not as fun as it used to be," Mom said. I was surprised, because I never thought she was having fun in those harried days of changing diapers, wiping noses, and washing dishes. I wondered whether she had in mind parts of life that a child doesn't see. Or whether, with time, even the hectic parts had taken on a shine, the way we come to miss even the things that annoyed us about a lost love.

We moved into the living room, where the carpet of my youth had been replaced with hardwood floors. I remembered the time I sat up all night on the carpet with a toothache. I started on the couch, but a little kid can't sit still with pain. With all the squirming and flailing, I kept ending up on the floor. Mom sat up with me, her crying on the shag carpet too.

A toothache isn't an emergency when there is no insurance, so we had to wait until we could get an appointment at the country dentist, who charged lower rates and extended credit. I learned that night that certain kinds of pain come in waves. When a wave comes on you can fear it and try to avoid it, but then it just hurts worse because you feel both the pain and the fear. Or you can lean into it and pay attention to how it feels as it washes over you. It diminishes a little, the way that a faint star seen in the corner of your eye disappears when you look straight at it.

Mom never talked about her childhood at all, except to say that she preferred to be an adult. One of the only stories she told me was that when she was in school, she was drinking from a water fountain when another girl—whose first and last name Mom remembered—pushed her head down into the fountain and knocked out her front tooth. There was no money to get it fixed, so she endured the missing tooth for years, careful to hide her smiles. When she turned seventeen and could get a job, the first thing she did was get the tooth fixed.

We were all healthy, so one of our biggest medical expenses was childbirth. Each one would take a couple of years to pay off, just in time for the next one. Dad joked that he had the house paid off before he had the children paid off. He would lie awake worrying at night, and he slept worse at the beginning of the school year, when we all wanted name-brand shoes and clothes. Buying the more expensive brand for one meant someone else had to make do with less. Vicki and I both needed braces, but they could afford only one. Vicki got the braces, because Dad said that looks mattered more for girls.

Our house was an enormous step up for Dad. He grew up a few miles away, in Knottsville, in a farmhouse with dirt floors. In the winter, snow would blow in under the wall planks. It was the 1940s, and the Tennessee Valley Authority was still in the process of bringing electricity to the rural South. Mr. Roosevelt's New Deal took a long time to reach our county. So Dad grew up without electricity or indoor plumbing. If we complained about sleeping two to a bed, he said we were lucky, because he had slept four to a bed. If we complained about waiting for the bathroom, he said try getting up in the middle of the night to go to the outhouse.

Dad can be a world-class bullshitter, but he did not exaggerate or romanticize his upbringing. He avoided talking about it, the way that some veterans avoid talking about their war. One story Dad told me stuck with me though. As a kid, he and a brother were at the general store. Other kids were hanging around there, eating peanuts and drinking bottles of Coca-Cola. A young man saw Dad looking longingly at the snacks and asked, "Are you Payne's boys?" They said they were. He said he knew they "had come up rough." He bought them a Coke and some peanuts, which Dad remembers the taste of today. I would think about that story when I hung around the truck stop. Dad always made sure I had a dollar or two for candy and fries.

If the highway defined our place on one side, it was the Ohio River that defined it on the other. Our backyard was a long strip of grass that turned into an acre of vegetable garden, where Dad spent all his time off. Beyond that was a little creek where I spent my time off. The creek had minnows and frogs, and now and then we would startle a rabbit and watch its white tail bound off through the woods. We learned to identify the hoofprints of deer that would drink from the creek, but they were too sly, or we were too noisy, to ever catch a glimpse of them. The neighbor kids and I used hatchets to chop down small trees and build log cabins the size of tents. One hot day I took a drink from the creek, but it tasted like shit and motor oil so I never did that again.

Beyond the creek lay fields of soybeans separated by strips of woods. I don't know who owned those fields. It was probably corporate farming, because there were no farmhouses and few barns around. In the fall, combines would show up on trucks, shave the fields down to stubble, and be gone the next day. So there were no farmers yelling at us kids to stay out of their fields. I treated it all, creek and fields and woods, as our backyard.

When the fields were freshly plowed, we could find arrowheads chipped from flint, some still sharp at the point. On the back end they had fine notches where they had been fastened to the arrow or spear. We imagined that the Native Americans had been there just before our parents bought the house. I later learned that the arrowheads could have been much older. The reason they were so common in that area is that they had been accumulating not for hundreds but for thousands of years. The last of the Native people in that area were forced out by the Indian Removal Act in 1830, though their numbers had already been decimated by fights with European settlers and the smallpox the settlers carried with them.

After crossing several fields, we would come to the river itself, huge and muddy and fast-moving, separating us from what seemed like a foreign land on the other side: Indiana. The North.

Living literally on the line between the North and South captured so much about our lives. We were clearly, obviously, and proudly southerners. Some kids played cops and robbers, others played cowboys and Indians, but we all played Civil War, and no one wanted to be the Yankees. And yet, even as kids we knew that our southernness was complicated. In school, we learned that our state had been neutral in the war, which is technically true. In reality, the state was torn apart by it. At the start of the war, President Lincoln called for the states to raise seventy-five thousand troops to stop the rebellion. Governor Beriah Magoffin responded that "Kentucky will furnish no troops for the wicked purpose of subduing her sister Southern states." Despite the official neutrality, young men formed militias and went to fight for both sides.

We learned in school that slavery was a great evil that was ended by the war. But we also learned that most people in the South did not own slaves and the reason they were fighting was that their land had been invaded by northerners. It was a provocation, we were told, that would lead anyone to defend themselves. We learned, with equal pride, that both Abraham Lincoln and Jefferson Davis were born in Kentucky. The teachers, like old Governor Magoffin, portrayed a strained neutrality, trying to avoid or delay outright hostilities.

Learning about these things animated our grade school minds more than other history topics. Maybe it was because we still felt the presence of the Civil War in our daily lives. Or maybe it was because it was fought in our own backyards. We asked our teachers questions about who was on which side and what happened in particular battles. But when we got into too much detail, the teachers grew nervous and changed the subject the way Mom did when I asked about the people in that car.

We learned that the Underground Railroad went through our town. I imagined it as a literal train that ran through tunnels under the ground. We were told that some of the old houses near the river had secret passages and tunnels in them to help the slaves escape. If they made it across the river to the North, they would be safe. In those stories, our Kentucky ancestors were always the good guys, helping the slaves escape across the river. It was many years later that I realized the reason anyone had to pass through secret doors and cross the river in skiffs in the dark of night was that most of our people were not on their side.

When I was a teenager, I was invited by an art teacher to help paint a mural on a downtown building. It featured Josiah Henson, a man who had been enslaved in our county before he escaped. In fact, our house is adjacent to the plot of land that was once Amos Riley's plantation, where Josiah Henson was enslaved. The background of the mural is full of colorful symbols of Kentucky. There are bright red cardinals and yellow goldenrod. The painting is arranged as a timeline. On the left, a woolly mammoth rises out of the mist of memory. From there, the Ohio River flows beneath a blue moon, tracing the path of history, of progress. In the middle, Josiah Henson stands in a triumphant pose, his arms outstretched and his fists clenched. He has a full white beard and a broad smile. He looks a little like Morgan Freeman. On the right, there is a kettle of burgoo, the local soup that is a little like gumbo, but made with smoked meat instead of seafood.

For years, I would point out to anyone who would listen that I helped paint it. The mural was part of a town-sponsored project to recognize our history. But then, as now, few people knew who he was. How Josiah came to live there, and how he left, is one of the greatest stories of emancipation that almost no one in my hometown seems to know.

Josiah was born in Port Tobacco, Maryland. His earliest reported memory was seeing his father enter their cabin and collapse on the dirt floor, covered in blood. His father's name is believed to have been Mason. Minutes earlier, Mason had been tied to a post and whipped by a blacksmith. At fifty lashes, the torturer stopped to check his vital signs. Satisfied that the man was strong enough to survive the whipping, the blacksmith continued to a hundred. At the end, the overseer nailed Mason's ear to the whipping post. The blacksmith cut it off, the ear still nailed to the post as Mason screamed and the crowd of White onlookers cheered. The overseer addressed the crowd: "That's what he gets for striking a White man!"

The White man in question was the overseer. Days earlier, he had ordered Celia, Mason's wife, to go work in a distant field. Once she was isolated, the overseer ambushed her. But the field was not far enough removed to silence her screams, and they brought Mason running. Mason beat the rapist, broke his nose and blackened his eyes and left him bloodied in the field as he ran to the woods, well aware of the punishment awaiting him. He hid in the woods, searching for food at night, but there was not enough to live on. Eventually the overseer's guards found him.

After his wounds healed, Mason was sold down the river. Today, "sold down the river" means to be betrayed. It comes from the practice of slavers sending people from the border states down the Ohio and Mississippi rivers to sell them into even more brutal conditions in the sprawling plantations of Mississippi, Alabama, and Louisiana. Josiah never saw his father again. He would be haunted for the rest of his life by the prospect of being sold down the river. However miserable his life was, however meager the food, and however brutal the overseer, there was always the specter of even greater cruelty down the river. Now Celia, Josiah, and his older brother, John, would have to survive together on their own.

They did, but only for a few years. When Josiah was around nine years old, everything changed. The man who enslaved them, Dr. McPherson, was out drinking one night. Riding home, he fell off his horse while crossing a stream. The stream was shallow, but he was too drunk; he could have simply stood up, but he drowned instead.

There was no one else to run his farm, so McPherson's heirs sold off his estate. That meant that Josiah, Celia, and John were put up for sale. The day of the auction, they were placed on the auction block one at a time. Josiah later wrote that when his brother was taken away, he tried to cry out, but he felt like his throat was swollen shut. Then Celia was torn from Josiah and placed on the auction block. A blacksmith named Isaac Riley made the highest bid, and Celia was ushered away. Then the auctioneer pulled Josiah onto the auction block. He could not see his mother or his brother. Josiah was purchased by Adam Robb, who did not own a plantation or even a farm. He specialized in trafficking children, buying them cheap when they were young and selling them for a higher price once they had grown.

Celia broke free from the man who had removed her from the auction block and pleaded with Isaac Riley to keep her little boy with her. He slapped her. She fell at his feet, crying and begging. He kicked her in the head and stomach and left her sobbing on the floor.

Josiah was taken to Robb's home and left in a cabin shared with dozens of other enslaved people. He lay down on a pile of rags in the corner on the dirt floor. He stayed there for days, crying for his mother, coughing, and losing weight. Realizing that he would make no money from his purchase if the boy died, Robb arranged to sell Josiah to Isaac Riley. They both expected that he would die. So Riley agreed to take him, and only if he lived would he repay Robb with some blacksmith work. Reunited with her son, Celia nursed him back to health. It was not the last time a brush with death would keep him with his family.

Josiah and Celia worked on Isaac Riley's Maryland farm from dawn to dark and slept in a one-room, dirt-floor cabin with several others. As Josiah grew, he became tall and muscular. His strength meant that he was favored in some ways by Riley, but it also meant that harder work fell on him.

When he was thirteen, a boy named William from a neighboring farm secretly learned to read and agreed to teach Josiah. They knew they had to be careful, but Josiah could not resist the possibility. He fashioned a pen out of a goose quill and made ink from charcoal. He collected fallen apples from the orchard and sold them to buy a spelling book for eleven cents. One morning when he was harnessing Riley's horse, the horse bolted and Josiah ran to catch him. In the commotion, his hat fell off and the spelling book that he had hidden there fell to the ground. Isaac Riley stamped it under the heel of his boot. He told Josiah to pick it up, and when he bent down, Riley hit him in the head with his cane. He beat Josiah until he lost consciousness. It was weeks before he recovered from the beating. The next time Riley saw him he said, "So you want to be a fine gentleman? Remember if you meddle with a book again I'll knock your brains out." William was sold down the river because he had tried to teach Josiah to read, and Josiah never heard from him again.

Despite the abuse, as Josiah entered his twenties he grew taller and stronger and more skilled at his work. He became a leader among the other enslaved workers, and Isaac Riley came to rely on him more and more. At one point, Josiah discovered that the overseer was stealing from Riley. He could not just report it to Riley, because Riley might not believe him, and if the overseer found out it would put Josiah's life in danger. Josiah tipped off Riley about when and where to be so he would catch the overseer in the act himself. It worked. In a surprising move, Riley assigned Josiah to replace the overseer, a role he kept for more than a decade. Josiah enjoyed the added status and respect. He used his position to obtain better food and conditions for the other enslaved workers when he could. But his new job would soon place him in a dilemma.

Isaac Riley's business was in trouble, and he was going into debt. On top of that, he fell into a dispute with his brother-in-law, who brought several lawsuits against him. One after another, Riley was losing the lawsuits, and he feared he would lose his farm. In desperation, he hatched a plan with his brother Amos Riley in Kentucky. He would send all his enslaved workers to Amos's plantation so that they could not be seized. Once he got his business affairs in order, Amos would send them back. Isaac charged Josiah with leading the group to Kentucky.

There were eighteen other people, plus Josiah's wife, Charlotte, and their two young sons. Isaac Riley signed a pass that gave them permission to travel, and they loaded a wagon with supplies. It would be a 650-mile journey for a group of people who had never traveled more than a few miles from the farms they called home. They left in February 1825. The wagon was not big enough for everyone, so the adults walked behind in the snow.

They traveled at night to avoid trouble and rested during the day. Even so, when they passed other people on the road, White men would sometimes stop them and ask to see their papers. When they reached the Ohio River, they sold the horse and wagon and bought a skiff to continue the rest of their journey by water.

Camping on the banks of the river near Cincinnati, they met a group of free Black people who invited the group to stay with them. The free people explained that Ohio was free soil, and tried to convince the party that they were now free. All they had to do was walk away from the river and begin new lives. But Josiah hesitated. For one thing, there were bands of slave catchers roaming northern states who would kidnap emancipated slaves and sell them back into slavery. And they would not take them back to Maryland or Kentucky—they would sell them down the river.

Even more powerful than these practical considerations, according to Josiah's later writings, was his conscience. He had ambitions to be free, but he had planned to buy his freedom from the Rileys, then purchase his family's freedom. Despite the cruelties of slavery and the abuse from Isaac Riley, Josiah still believed that following Isaac's orders was the honorable thing. He thought of the sermons he had heard about the great chain of being and how everyone, from angels to humans to animals, had their rightful place in the order of things. He thought of the preacher's admonitions that it was his duty to obey his "master" in all things and that it was God's will that Black people should be enslaved to White people. Although he knew that slavery was wrong, he also believed that it would be wrong of him to escape.

Josiah's inability to break free of slavery's warped moral teachings calls to mind Huckleberry Finn's famous reckoning with his conscience. When his friend Jim, the escaped slave, gets caught, Huck has to decide whether to let him be returned or to break him out. At first, he decides to do the "honorable" thing and let Jim's enslavers know where to find him. When he makes that decision, he feels suddenly cleansed of guilt: "I felt good and all washed clean of sin for the first time I had ever felt so in my life, and I knowed I could pray now." But he gets to thinking about his time with Jim as a person and as a friend, and he realizes he cannot abandon him. "All right, then, I'll go to hell," he says, accepting that he would rather "take up wickedness" than abandon Jim. On the banks of

Cincinnati, Josiah was not able to take up the wickedness necessary to deliver his family and their eighteen followers to freedom. Not yet. It would take two more betrayals by the Rileys to shake his faith.

They continued their journey, until in April they climbed out of the boat on the landing at Amos Riley's plantation. Crossing the fields where I used to hunt for arrowheads, they walked to the farmhouse and reported to Amos. They worked on Amos Riley's plantation for three years. During that time, Josiah became a well-regarded preacher, preaching to other enslaved people on Sundays and memorizing the Bible passages he heard from other preachers, because he still could not read.

After three years, Isaac Riley contacted his brother in Kentucky. But he did not call them home. Instead, he instructed Amos to keep Josiah and his family but sell the others down the river. Josiah was anguished that he had not freed them when he had the chance. But now there was nothing he could do. He watched helplessly as his friends were separated from one another and sold south.

Although Josiah had not been sold south, he knew his time was running out if he was ever going to be free. He hatched a plan, with the help of an abolitionist preacher, to earn enough money to finally buy his freedom. He would travel back to Maryland to visit Isaac, collecting donations for preaching along the way. By the time he arrived at Isaac Riley's farm, he hoped to have several hundred dollars. To his surprise, Amos Riley did not object when Josiah asked to visit Isaac. Josiah had been so dependable for so long that Amos trusted him, and he wrote a pass to allow Josiah to travel.

Josiah had earned enough money preaching to buy a horse and wagon and new clothes. When he arrived at Isaac Riley's Maryland farm, he sold the horse and wagon and had $350 to buy his freedom.

Isaac seemed glad to see Josiah again, but he also remarked on his fancy new clothes. He still could not stand to see Josiah acting like a "fine gentleman." The men negotiated, and Isaac eventually agreed to let Josiah purchase his freedom for $450—the $350 cash plus a promissory note for $100 more. Josiah headed back to Kentucky, full of joy, to tell his family and to earn the remaining $100. Once he was free, it would be easier to earn the money to buy their freedom too.

It was too good to be true. By the time he got back to Kentucky, Isaac had notified Amos of the deal. But he had added a zero to the promissory note. Now Josiah would have to earn $1,000, a nearly impossible burden. Before long, Amos ordered Josiah to accompany his son, Amos Junior, on a boat trip down the Mississippi to sell some goods. By the time they arrived in New Orleans, it had become clear that Josiah was the last of the property to be sold.

Josiah had reached a breaking point. Again and again he had done what he saw as the honorable thing. He could have run away so many times, but he didn't. And still, the Rileys took advantage of him and betrayed him. Now he was being sold down the river, never to see his family again. He silently resolved not to let himself be sold in New Orleans.

One night while Amos Junior and the three sailors on the boat slept, Josiah picked up an axe and stood over them in the sleeping cabin. He had already thought through how he could sink the boat. Now, his axe raised, he mapped out the order in which he would have to kill all four of them before the last one woke up.

Once again, his conscience would not let him go through with it. He put down the axe.

Josiah was slated to be sold the following day. That's when another brush with death intervened. This time, it was Amos Junior's. The young man woke in the night with terrible stomach pains. His health declined quickly throughout the next day, likely due to malaria. If he was going to live to return up the Mississippi, he needed Josiah. So Amos Junior canceled the sale, and Josiah nursed him back to health as the steamboat paddled slowly back to the Kentucky plantation.

Josiah knew then that the time had come. Charlotte sewed a sack to hang over Josiah's shoulders to carry their children. They now had three sons, one old enough to walk and two young enough to be carried. Josiah and Charlotte's cabin was not far from the muddy Ohio. They crossed the river in a skiff one night in September 1830 and walked away, like they had thought about doing so many times before.

Although it was a free state, southern Indiana was not safe territory. They had to travel at night to avoid the slave catchers. The sack full of children dug into Josiah's shoulders. They went days without meals. But they kept walking, all the way to Canada. Josiah Henson would go on to become a prominent abolitionist speaker and preacher and to found a school and a colony, called Dawn, for freed people in Canada. He became a part of the growing network of activists that today we call the Underground Railroad. It had taken years, but finally Josiah reoriented his conscience away from loyalty to White men's property rights and toward illegal freedom.

He took that journey between Canada and the Ohio River many more times to rescue people. One of them was his brother, John. By Josiah's count, he emancipated 118 people. He did not rest until he rescued 100 people—plus 18—the number he delivered to Amos Riley in Kentucky.

Harriet Beecher Stowe would later say that Josiah was one of a number of people on whom she based Uncle Tom. In Maceo, that seems to be the main interest in Josiah. There is a bronze historic marker where Amos Riley's plantation stood that reads, "Uncle Tom Lived Here." But to me, that tangential connection to fame is the least interesting thing about Josiah Henson. In the years since I learned about Henson's escape from the Riley plantation, I often wondered how living in their shadow shaped the world that I, my family, and my hometown inherited. Did playing in the same fields that Josiah plowed have any impact on the way we see the world? And if my brothers and I inherited anything from this history, was it from Josiah, the protagonist I identify with in my mind? Or was it from the Rileys, the White men with whom we have more in common?

This book is about how our circumstances—accidents of time, place, and history—set us on different paths, and how we bend our view of the world to make sense of it from where we stand. One of the circumstances that matters a great deal is the racial group we are born into. With two hundred years of hindsight it is easy to see Josiah as the hero and the Rileys as the villains. But some of today's most intense battles are over racial inequality, the long shadow of slavery, and whether we have come far enough from those days. The circumstances that divide us are about social class, and whether the insurance to fix a toothache is something every child ought to have. Our divisions are about religion, and the way that evangelical Christians turned down a new path in the last half century, the way Mom headed away from our old church toward her new Pentecostal passion. Our divisions are about cities versus small towns, and whether we find our community in sidewalk cafés or truck stop diners.

My town, like America itself, has always been conflicted about who exactly we are. There will be some energetic young teacher who just moved back home after college or some recently elected town council member. They will have an idea to link our town with Josiah, with the Underground Railroad, with those hidden passages in the old houses by the river. And then other parts of the community will push back and find a way to say, no, that is not who we are.

What must the townspeople have thought about that mural as they drove by it each day? This proud Black man, smiling as they passed. Were there complaints to the arts council? Letters to the editor? On a recent visit home, I went to see the mural of Josiah that I had helped paint so many years ago. I passed by the courthouse and noticed that the Confederate monument that stood there throughout my childhood had been removed. Only the granite base remained, with the inscription "To our Confederate heroes." Maybe my town was changing, I thought.

On the next block, there was the mural, the cardinals a little faded, on the side of the insurance company building. Except something was missing. Josiah had been painted entirely out of the picture. As I stood there in front of the faded mural, Josiah's absence felt like a betrayal. Now the focus of the mural, between the mists of memory and the steaming pot of burgoo, was a paddleboat. The kind that had been used to sell him, and so many others, down the river.

TWO

WHY YOU CAN'T REASON
WITH THEM
The Psychological Immune System

So convenient a thing it is to be a Reasonable
Creature, *since it enables one to find or make a
reason for every thing one has a mind to do.*

—BENJAMIN FRANKLIN

A few weeks after the 2020 election, I asked Brad in a Facebook conversation if he believed Donald Trump lied about the election being stolen from him. As soon as I posted the question I regretted it, because I dreaded the answer. On the one hand, I knew that my brother was a committed Trump supporter. On the other hand, I knew him to be a smart and sane person. I really wanted to know what he believed, and yet I was afraid of what he would say, because I didn't know how I could relate to him if he embraced Trump's lie on this most fundamental question of American democracy.

He seemed to feel the tension, too, and tried to avoid the

subject. He said, "You're my brother and I love you. I'm not going to have a semantic debate with you."

"I love you too," I said, not able to let it go, "but it's not a semantic debate. It's not a matter of opinion. It's an issue of fact that divides reality-based people from delusional loons. You can admit that you don't like Biden and also that Trump lied about losing the election." In the meantime, someone I don't know chimed in to say that the election was stolen, and if I can't see that, my brain doesn't function properly. Then Brad surprised me. He said, "By the letter of the law, yes, Biden won. I think there was some malfeasance there in areas, I do. But it can't be proven." I figured that was as close as he was going to get to admitting that Biden was the legitimate president. So I thanked him for his honesty and let it drop.

It was a fascinating example of the ways that people use reason flexibly to defend their identities and commitments. Trump's false claims about the election being stolen put Trump supporters in a real bind. They wanted to believe it. It certainly felt wrong to them that Joe Biden won the election. And yet, dozens of court cases, recounts, and voting audits indicated again and again that the vote tallies were correct. How to resolve this conflict? Some seemed to disregard all the evidence that the election was fair and fully embraced Trump's claims, like the fellow who opined about my brain function. Brad, on the other hand, reached a different conclusion. Biden won by the letter of the law (but not the spirit, presumably). It was a mere technicality, like a criminal who is really guilty but got off because of some procedural error by the police. Or more likely, Brad's reference was to the Pharisees in Paul's second letter to the Corinthians, who rule by the letter of the law as opposed to the spirit of the law animating Jesus and his followers. The malfeasance couldn't be proven, but it was out there somewhere, lurking like alligators in a swamp. This solution allowed him to come to terms with the evidence that was being broadcast on all the mainstream news sources and, to a lesser extent, even conservative news outlets. And yet, he was able to hold on to the larger feeling that Biden's victory was, deep down, illegitimate.

Flexible reasoning is a bipartisan affair. A few months before the election, I caught myself doing some mental gymnastics of my own. Tara Reade had accused Joe Biden of sexual assault. When I heard the news on the radio, standing in my kitchen, my heart sank. Would this mean four more years of Trump? But my next thought was that she was probably lying. There didn't seem to be any hard evidence, so she had not proven her case, I decided. Then I remembered how I had argued, during the approval hearing for Brett Kavanaugh, that we should take the claims of women who allege sexual harassment or assault seriously even if they can't produce evidence. Okay, I replied to myself, we should take her claim seriously, but it's still just her word against his. And, I reasoned, the worst-case scenario would be that we have two men, both accused of sexual assault, running for president (and anyway, Trump was accused by way more women than Biden was). This elaborate debate unfolded over about ten seconds while I rinsed the coffee pot. Before the coffee brewed, I was once again comfortable that I didn't need to change my preference or my vote. The story soon fell out of the news. I rarely thought about it and quickly began to forget the details. I had to look up Tara Reade's name to write this.

Not changing, of course, is what motivated these convoluted trains of thought for both me and Brad. We knew where we wanted to end up and just needed the right chain of thought to get there. This chapter explores how people reason flexibly in defense of the ideas and identities that are important to them. We will see how many of the apparent flaws in human reasoning—like logical inconsistencies, flip-flopping over time, applying different standards to your own side's arguments than to the other side's—aren't really flaws but features. Our cognitive systems are doing just what they are set up to do, which is not always to seek truth.

THERE ARE REASONS, AND THEN THERE ARE CAUSES FOR REASONS

We ordinarily make sense of people's behavior based on their reasons. We all share this folk theory, which says that people form reasons—beliefs, desires, intentions—and then act on them. Dad goes to the grocery because he *intends* to cook dinner tonight. He takes an umbrella because he *believes* it might rain. But we also know people sometimes make up reasons after the fact to justify what they've done for other reasons. Mom has been working too hard, she says, cleaning up the shards from Dad's dropped whiskey glass.

Reasons are important. We judge intentional harm more harshly than accidental harm. We judge selfish motives more harshly than cluelessness. And when someone does something that seems puzzling or senseless, we want to know what they were thinking. But we have to go a step further if we really want to explain human behavior. People have their reasons, but those reasons have *causes*.

The causes of people's reasons are even more important than the reasons themselves when we try to understand why people act the way they do. Some people prefer to increase safety-net spending because they *believe* it will reduce inequality and they *want* more equality. Others prefer to reduce safety-net spending because they *believe* it will encourage hard work and self-reliance and they *value* those traits. But why do different people believe and want and value such different things? We need to start with something more fundamental than politics: the pursuit of happiness itself.

Most of the choices we make in life are because we think we will be happier with one kind of outcome than another. Psychologists Daniel Gilbert and Timothy Wilson have spent years studying how we predict our future feelings, and why those predictions are so often mistaken. One of the main reasons is that we fail to notice all the mental work we do on a daily basis to keep us feeling fine. Sports fans predict that they will be devastated if their team loses to their rival and that their anguish will last for days. In reality, when their team goes down in defeat they feel mildly annoyed for an afternoon and by the next day are back to feeling normal. The same pattern holds for bigger life events. Professors think that if they are denied tenure and lose their jobs it will ruin their life. But a few months after it happens, the former academics are as happy as they were beforehand. Lovers expect that if they get dumped, it will be a crushing experience that changes them forever. But in reality, the vast majority of people bounce back to normal within a couple of months.

It's not that we are indifferent to these events. To the contrary, when something upsetting happens, we mobilize a massive defense against it. Psychologists call the set of thought processes we use to protect our own well-being the psychological immune system. And it works. When our team loses, we blame the referees or bad luck, or we can simply put today's game behind us and start looking forward to the next one, when we will really show them. Being denied tenure has a way of suddenly illuminating how much better paying and less stressful a nonacademic job might be. Even getting dumped, though painful in the short term, leads people to appreciate how many other fish there are in the sea and how much they enjoy their new freedom. Eventually we might find a way to be grateful, because if that person had not dumped us we would not have the cherished relationship or children or life we have today. So when we imagine experiencing one of these events, we think about how it would feel, but we neglect how our psychological immune system will swing into action to protect and restore our well-being over time.

The basic observation that people use motivated reasoning to protect their psychological well-being is one of the most consistent findings in all of psychology. Motivated reasoning is usually seen as a flaw in human rationality, because it makes us logically inconsistent and sometimes intellectually dishonest. One of the easiest ways to collect Likes on social media is to point out some hypocrisy you have spotted in your opponents. And it is easy to do, because people are incredibly inconsistent. The principle that partisans invoke when talking about one issue will be contradicted when talking about another issue. Democrats like to point out that Republicans claim to be "pro-life" when it comes to banning abortion but not when imposing the death penalty. Republicans note that Democrats claim to be "tolerant" of racial and cultural differences but not of evangelical Christian beliefs. It is easy for either side to argue that these cases are different for various reasons, so that they are not really contradicting themselves at all. But that is part of my point: life is complex enough that we can find a justification for nearly any position we want to hold. And for every contradiction, we can find a reason why it's not really a contradiction, because the cases are different in some way. The mental gymnastics that people perform are not an aberration but a normal part of the way people think.

Take, for example, a study that asked participants to evaluate two welfare policies, one of which provided generous benefits and the other, much less generous. In general, Democrats would be expected to support the generous policy and Republicans to prefer the less generous one. But this study also varied which party was said to be proposing the policies. One group read that Democrats proposed the generous policy, as might be expected. The other group read that the Republicans proposed the more generous policy and Democrats favored the stingy one. When party information was included, Democrats strongly preferred whichever policy the Democrats proposed, and Republicans preferred whatever Republicans proposed. Party mattered much more than the actual policy substance. Scads of studies like this have been done, and the results are almost always the same. A review paper examined more than fifty studies of politically motivated reasoning and found that partisan-motivated reasoning was consistent, and it was symmetrical for Democrats and Republicans. The authors gave the paper the rather discouraged sounding title "At Least Bias Is Bipartisan."

These mental gymnastics often lead us to take positions that are at odds with reason and evidence. But that's not because they are flaws in rationality. Rather, it is because our cognitive systems value self-protection, sometimes more than reason. Like the biological immune system, the psychological immune system is constantly humming away in the background whether we notice it or not, ready to pounce at the first sign of a threat.

To see how this plays out in real time, consider studies of how people experience something as innocuous as vacations. When researchers asked college students who were about to go on vacation how pleasant they expected it to be, they rated it very highly. That's not surprising, because if they did not expect to have fun they probably would not have planned that vacation. But when researchers beeped them at random times during the vacation itself, they were not having as much fun as they thought they would. Most people rated their real-time experiences as only middling. A lot of vacation, after all, consists of taking transportation, waiting in lines, or doing supposedly fun things that are a little disappointing. And yet, when vacationers returned home and researchers asked them to look back and rate their experience, they once again rated it as very positive. So the experiences morphed from "This is gonna be amazing!" to "This is fine" to "That was amazing!"

The reason is that when people reflected on their vacation experiences, they were selective. They ignored the boring train ride and the annoying crowds and remembered that one perfect sunset, that one amazing meal, or that one romantic moment. Their psychological immune systems were at work. If they had not had those particular experiences to support a positive memory, they could have found others. They did not objectively weigh their experiences and then pronounce them as good or bad. Instead they considered how they wanted to feel about the vacation and then found the evidence they needed to back it up.

Here's the most important part of the study: When researchers asked vacationers whether they would go on a similar trip again, the best predictor of their plans was not their real-time experience. It was their remembered experience, the one that was patched together in rosy hindsight. The bulk of the vacationers' actual experience was sealed within a memory bubble that was inaccessible once the vacation was over.

The same thing happens not only for experiences like vacations but also for beliefs and ideas. Repeated studies have found that when experimenters are successful at changing research participants' opinions about an issue, the participants rarely admit that they had been wrong. Instead, they misremember their prior opinion as if they had believed their current opinion all along. All of us feel as if we are right about most topics most of the time. We can't all be right, of course. But from the inside, the experience really is very convincing. Every time we reach for evidence to support our views, it is easily at hand. And if we were ever wrong about something in the past, it seems to have slipped our mind.

Studies like this make you wonder how much of our own past is a distorted memory. How much truth are we giving up for the sake of pleasant memories? And is it worth the cost of deluding ourselves that way? On this last point, the answer appears to be a clear *yes*. We deploy the psychological immune system because it is incredibly effective. People who are more adept at using mental gymnastics to defend themselves tend to be happier, more optimistic, and more resilient to stress. In fact, one of the only groups so far identified as lacking self-serving mental gymnastics is a group you don't want to belong to. They are the clinically depressed.

Fortunately most people, most of the time, are not clinically depressed, in part because we are hard at work making ourselves feel better. Our psychological immune systems are not, however, just used for retroactively enjoying mediocre vacations. The deeper purpose is to protect our identity—the conviction that deep down, no matter how many awful things we have said or done, we are good and reasonable people.

THE GOOD, TRUE SELF

Being a good person is at the heart of people's sense of identity. When psychologist Nina Strohminger and philosopher Shaun Nichols teamed up to study how people understand the "true self," they found it was moral qualities, more than any other, that made people who they are. For centuries, scholars have argued that memory is critical to a continuous sense of self. If you wake up one morning with complete amnesia about your life up to that moment, most people would agree that, in some real sense, you have lost your identity. But Strohminger and Nichols found that changes in morality are even more important than memory. Here is how one of their studies went.

Imagine that Jim is in a car accident and sustains a brain injury. He is taken to the hospital, where he has brain surgery. When he recovers, he is healthy, but the brain surgery has changed him in some specific ways. In one condition of the study, Jim is now amnesiac and cannot remember anything that happened to him in his life before the accident. In another condition, he has lost all his desires. He is apathetic and uninterested in things he used to care about. And in another condition, he has lost his moral conscience. He can no longer judge right from wrong and is not moved by the suffering of others. After reading one of these scenarios, study participants were asked whether the patient is still really *Jim*. The researchers found that changes to his morality made him seem like a different person more than changes in memories or desires.

The researchers followed up this study of hypothetical scenarios with a more realistic version to understand how these changes play out in people's lives. Anyone who has lost a loved one to dementia knows that part of the pain of witnessing their decline is the feeling that the person we knew and loved is slipping away even while they are still alive. Strohminger and Nichols surveyed participants in support groups for people caring for a loved one with dementia. Dementia is not a single disease, but a variety of conditions that can result from different diseases, like Alzheimer's, ALS, and strokes. Some kinds affect mainly memory, while others can also change people's emotions and personalities in profound ways. The researchers asked respondents to rate the extent to which their loved one was experiencing changes in various areas, including memory, personality traits, language, and morality.

It was changes in morality more than any other traits that made respondents feel that their loved one was no longer the same person. The loved one might have massively impaired memory, failing to recognize their own family members. They might even have personality changes, becoming less creative or more sociable, but those changes did not make them seem like a different person. Changes in moral traits like trustworthiness or compassion, though, left family members feeling they no longer knew the person.

Studies show that when people hear about a drug addict who has gotten clean, they think he has rediscovered his true self. But when he falls off the wagon, he has lost sight of his true self. Hardly anyone seems to think that when an addict indulges in their favorite drug, they are expressing their true inner addict. Liars, ne'er-do-wells, even murderers are perceived as turning away from their true selves when they do bad things. The true self is almost always perceived to be morally good if you go deep enough. This finding has been replicated in many cultures around the world. Surprisingly, even misanthropes see people's true selves as good.

If being a good person is at the heart of what we mean by the true self for other people, it is even more powerful for how we understand our own true selves. Scores of studies have found that people rate themselves as consistently morally good. Even people imprisoned for violent crimes view themselves as good people. According to one study, they rate themselves not only as kinder and more compassionate than other prisoners but also as morally superior to the average community member. If violent criminals manage to keep up a good opinion of themselves, it is even easier for the rest of us to overlook our more mundane flaws and failures to see ourselves as basically good people.

But our high opinions of ourselves are not about ourselves alone. We extend those high opinions to groups we belong to. Forming a tight connection between your identity and a group is what defines really belonging to a group. Everyone belongs, in a shallow sense, to an unlimited number of groups. You might belong to the group of people with brown hair, aging punk rockers, people shorter than six feet four, and so on. Internet communities with thousands of members exist for people who like to chew ice, those who film elevators opening and closing, and people who use photo editing to create pictures of birds with arms. But sharing a characteristic or an interest with these groups doesn't by itself mean someone belongs to the group. What really matters is whether their identity is bound up with the group. Understanding how identities make groups meaningful, and how groups create identities, requires diving into one of the most important and most misunderstood studies in the history of psychology: the minimal group.

Henri Tajfel was born to a Jewish family in Poland in 1919. Because Jews were not allowed to attend university in Poland, he went to the Sorbonne in France (where he changed his name to Henri from Hersz). When Germany invaded Poland to ignite the Second World War, he could not go home, so he fought with the French army. He was deployed for about a year. One night after the sounds of battle faded, he crawled into the woods for a few hours' sleep. Awakened by a German bayonet, he was taken prisoner. On the long march to the prison camp, he slowly ate his Polish passport and any papers that identified him. In the prison camp he pretended to be a Frenchman, because if the Germans found out he was a Polish Jew, he would surely have been killed.

One half of the camp was French and English soldiers, and the other half was Russians. Conditions were hard for everyone, but most on the French and English side managed to survive. The Russian camp was worked and starved to the point that around half of the prisoners died. Henri survived the prison camp for five long years. When the war was over, he returned to his hometown in Poland to find that his entire family, and nearly everyone he knew, had been killed in the concentration camps.

Reflecting later on his experience, he tried to make sense of why group labels that meant so little to him had such an enormous influence on his fate. Why was he barred from university in Poland but not in France? Why, as a prisoner of war, was he allowed to live if he was a Frenchman but not if he was a Polish Jew? Why did nationality mean that most people in his camp survived while half of the Russian soldiers died? And why would the same German guards whom he chatted and smoked cigarettes with as individuals have easily killed him if they had been given the order?

The two decades following the war were formative for the emerging field of social psychology. Its founders, many of whom were themselves Jewish refugees from Europe, were animated by the quest to understand how people who were generally decent to one another as individuals could be turned into opposing armies who would willingly engage in such a global cataclysm. In the Allied countries, the quest took the form of trying to understand the roots of Nazi depravity.

Some scholars were inclined toward personality-based explanations. Theodore Adorno and Else Frenkel-Brunswik (Jewish refugees from Germany and Austria) developed a personality scale they called the F-scale (for the fascist personality). It had questions like "Obedience and respect for authority are the most important virtues children should learn," and "People can be divided into two distinct classes: the weak and the strong." These scholars adopted a Freudian view, in which children raised by harsh and domineering parents redirected their rage toward their parents onto the outside world. As a result, they viewed social life as a ruthless competition for dominance. The only way to prevent chaos, in this worldview, is to make sure that everyone sticks to their allotted social roles and that norm breakers are punished harshly. These scholars suspected that German culture and child-rearing practices made them especially prone to fascist thinking. Their work became known as the "authoritarian personality theory."

Other scholars looked for answers in the power of situations. Stanley Milgram devised his famous obedience experiments, in which a researcher elicited appalling degrees of obedience from participants by calmly insisting, "the experiment requires that you continue." The obedience studies were an attempt to understand how rank-and-file German soldiers could be led to carry out mass atrocities simply by following orders. In the process, Milgram revealed that most people—not just Germans—are vastly more obedient to authority than anyone suspected. Solomon Asch showed that an authority in a lab coat was not even necessary to coax people into going along. He found that if several peers said something that was plainly false, the majority of people would conform and recite an obvious lie. Asch's study was an early indication that people often care more about fitting in than finding truth.

This was the background against which Henri Tajfel began his career as a psychologist in England. As he tried to make sense of his experience in the war, as well as the ongoing conflict over civil rights in the United States, the troubles in Northern Ireland, and the various ethnic and nationalist conflicts roiling Europe, he was convinced something was missing from the standard explanations. The personality explanation was not enough, because group conflicts had a way of leading entire populations, including even mild-mannered people, into combative thinking. He found the situational pressures toward conformity to be more convincing but still incomplete. Why, for example, do people eagerly conform to certain authorities but not others? He noticed that wealthy Slovenians had the same stereotypes about poor Bosnians that the English had about Pakistani immigrants and that White Americans had about Black Americans. Why did powerful groups consistently come to see less powerful groups as lazy, unintelligent, and prone to crime? Some aspects of group conflicts seemed incredibly particular while others seemed universal.

Tajfel argued that the answer lies in the nature of social groups themselves. We don't obey just any authority, and we don't conform to just any norms. We want to walk in lockstep with *our people*, not just any people. And to do that, we differentiate ourselves from the other people. But who counts as our people?

The groups that really matter, Tajfel argued, are the ones that create and sustain our sense of identity as a good and valuable person. You can tell which groups matter by whether you feel attacked when someone insults or criticizes that group. When someone says, "Men can be such jerks," some men feel the urge to respond, "But not *all* men are jerks!" That defensiveness is a sign that they felt personally criticized when the category of "men" was criticized. That connection between the group and the self suggests the group is a meaningful in-group. Some groups are more meaningful than others, and some people are more attached to certain groups than others. But even trivial-seeming groups can still evoke a surprisingly strong emotional reaction.

When I was in graduate school in St. Louis, I went to a Cardinals game with some friends. I don't remember much about the game, but I remember the crowd rushing out of the stadium at the end. I had taken the Metro to the stadium, and the platform soon became crowded as thousands of rowdy fans flooded the terminal, waiting to squeeze into the train cars. The loud buzz of voices started to take on a rhythmic beat—boom boom BOOM, boom boom BOOM. Then I noticed that the two sides of the terminal, one going east and the other going west, were taking turns. Were they singing to each other? Not quite. As the voices became more distinct, I heard the chant ringing out: "East side sucks!" "West side sucks!" As it swelled and grew, the chant swallowed up everyone on both sides of the station. Suddenly I found myself chanting along, insulting strangers for no good reason and loving it.

No one had planned or organized it, but we somehow all followed a set of rules. We forgot about the shared allegiance we had for the past three hours as the vast majority of us had cheered on the Cardinals. Now the groups that defined us were simply being on the east side or west side of the terminal. We even took turns, each side quietly pausing to be insulted when it was the other side's turn to say we sucked. All these years later, it still feels a little mysterious how that moment spontaneously happened. All I know is that east side really sucked.

Tajfel was the first to show how trivial a group can be and still evoke a psychological reaction. He divided a sample of teenage boys into two groups based on whether they overestimated or underestimated the number of dots in a picture. In another version of the study he divided them based on whether they preferred a painting by Paul Klee or Wassily Kandinsky. Once they knew which group they were in, the boys did not get a chance to come together as a group. Instead, they went to cubicles to fill out a survey. On the survey, the boys indicated that people in the other group (the out-group) were more similar to one another than the individuals in the in-group. They rated the boys in the in-group more likable than those in the out-group. And when they were asked to divide up money between the groups, they kept more for their in-group than the out-group.

According to Tajfel's longtime collaborator John Turner, he did not really expect such trivial group assignments to create the kind of group favoritism that it did. Tajfel's original aim was to establish a baseline against which real groups could be compared. But instead, even these silly groups led to a significant degree of special treatment for the in-group and denigration of the out-group. The effect is powerful. I have replicated it many times in classroom demonstrations with college students. Underestimators quickly assume that they are the realistic and cautious group, and hence smarter and better than the overestimators. Overestimators, on the other hand, assume that they are optimistic and positive people, and hence better than the dreary underestimators. Minimal groups don't stay minimal. However meaningless the groups begin, people find a way to add meaning to them.

This is where the minimal group study is so often misunderstood. Today's readers often take the point to be that simply being divided into groups, even flimsy ones, can explain why people engage in intergroup conflict. But Tajfel's thinking was always about real groups, thick groups that had a hold on people's identities and sense of meaning. In the back of his mind was always the question of why being a Frenchman saved his life while being a Polish Jew got everyone he loved murdered. It was most definitely not because of some trivial categorization exercise.

No, Tajfel's point was that the act of thinking of oneself as a group member was critical. To understand why Slovenians thought Bosnians were lazy or White Americans thought the same about Black Americans, you didn't need to look into the personal characteristics of the Slovenians, the Bosnians, or the White or Black Americans. You only needed to understand what the groups were in those societies and which groups were advantaged or disadvantaged. If even trivial labels can instigate a mild level of group "conflict," think how much more powerful groups to which we really feel connected must be. Groups like race, religion, and nationality tie our concept of belonging to the group to our concept of being a good person. They attach our small individual lives to a history and a purpose larger than ourselves. Because of that, they give us a sense of meaning and mission that few other parts of life can rival. At the same time, these thick social groups mean that whatever we do on behalf of our group, we do in service of a greater good. These are *maximal* groups. If we are willing to discriminate against people based on counting dots, and if we are willing to yell insults at strangers across a train platform, how far are we willing to go when our notions of God and country and justice are on the line?

The answer, of course, is that many of us would do literally anything when acting on behalf of our most important groups. We would die, we would kill, and we would put on uniforms and fight against strangers who did nothing to us personally, because it was demanded by our groups.

As soon as we draw a boundary that defines our in-groups, we have also defined our out-groups on the other side of that line. And the more intensely devoted we are to our groups, the more antagonistic we are to outsiders. In a study led by psychologist Taya Cohen, the researchers looked at data gathered by anthropologists throughout the last century about hundreds of preindustrial civilizations around the world. They found that the more a civilization valued loyalty to their own group, the more warlike they were and the more they valued violence against other groups. Being a morally virtuous member of your groups and being a nightmare to out-groups are two sides of the same coin.

Tajfel's theory, and the research it gave rise to, led to the discovery of two basic psychological principles that virtually everyone employs. Understanding these principles helps today's political divisions make so much more sense. They are a set of nonnegotiable assumptions that we make about ourselves and the world, and every new experience or piece of information we encounter has to be made to fit with these assumptions. Together, these assumptions make up what I call the "psychological bottom line." The first nonnegotiable principle is that *I am a good and reasonable person.* The second principle is that *My groups are good and reasonable people.* When the psychological immune system protects us from threats, it does it by finding a way to make everything else add up to the psychological bottom line.

THE PSYCHOLOGICAL
BOTTOM LINE

The psychological bottom line is easy to achieve because of what psychologists call the "cognitive response principle." The principle says that no one changes their beliefs or attitudes based on information they receive. If they change, it is because of their own thoughts in response to the new information. For example, imagine a toothpaste advertisement that says their product will make your teeth 20 percent whiter. One person sees the ad and thinks about how they would like to have whiter teeth. Another sees the ad and thinks that it is probably misleading, then they think about other misleading marketing claims they've heard about, like how tobacco companies for years claimed their products were healthy stress relievers when they knew that they caused cancer. The first person will like the toothpaste brand more after seeing the ad than before, because they have generated positive thoughts about it. The second person won't like the toothpaste more; in fact they may even like it less than if they had never seen the ad at all, because they have now generated negative thoughts about the brand. The cognitive response principle, in short, says that all persuasion is self-persuasion. Any message we send to other people is simply an occasion for them to listen to their own thoughts in response.

Our own thoughts turn out to be inevitably encouraging and refreshingly reassuring about our own perspective whenever our social identities are involved. One popular idea in the early study of motivated reasoning was that people simply ignored information that was inconvenient for their existing beliefs or desires. But that turned out to be wrong. When people are confronted with inconvenient information, they think more, not less. Their psychological immune system revs up, and they start spinning lots of ideas to defend themselves. And then, following the cognitive response principle, they believe their own thoughts rather than the original information that was presented to them.

To test just how persuasive people find themselves, researchers asked participants to solve logic puzzles and make an argument to explain their answer. The experimenters later showed participants their own answers and arguments again, and asked them if they still believed they were true. They overwhelmingly accepted their own arguments as true whether they were actually correct or incorrect. In a second condition, the experimenters showed participants the arguments that other participants had made. Now they were much more skeptical, rejecting more than half of them. The most interesting condition was a third one, in which the experimenters showed participants the arguments that they had generated themselves, but labeled them as another participant's arguments. In this case, they rejected more than half of their own arguments as wrong. Suddenly, they could see the logical flaws that were invisible when they thought the argument was their own. This study shows why the content of the arguments doesn't always matter. If we think the argument comes from ourselves, we assume it is valid and don't think much more about it. But if it comes from someone else, we think hard and we lean toward skepticism.

In general, this tendency to believe our own thoughts is sensible and adaptive. Most of the thoughts we have as we go about our lives are true, and they have our own best interest at heart. By the time you finish breakfast you've probably had hundreds of ordinary thoughts that turned out to be trustworthy, from how to make the coffee to where you left your pants. As an individual thinker, it makes sense to trust our own thoughts. But if we *only* trusted our own thoughts, we would never learn anything. Learning involves a kind of trust, in which we allow our own thoughts to travel along with what a teacher is saying. The best teachers guide learners along a path of discovery so that the learner's own inner thoughts create the crucial aha moment. That's why the Socratic method of teaching by asking questions is so effective: it harnesses the power of the cognitive response principle.

Learning new information is much harder, though, once the psychological immune system gets involved. If you combine the psychological immune system with our tendency to believe in our own thoughts, it is easy to see how people can easily convince themselves that whatever they want to believe is true. Take the election fraud narrative, for example. For a committed Trump supporter, which of the two sets of ideas will feel more true:

1. I am a good and reasonable person.
2. The individuals in my group are good and reasonable people.
3. The leader of my group is lying to try to stay in power despite losing the election.

OR

1. I am a good and reasonable person.
2. The individuals in my group are good and reasonable people.
3. The leader of my group is defending us against our enemy's attempt to steal the election.

The second set of statements will not only ring truer, but it will also draw out different cognitive responses. The second will elicit affirming thoughts, whereas the first will prompt counterarguments. When new evidence is introduced, like dozens of court cases and recounts that failed to find voter fraud, it is always possible to generate more counterarguments, even if they are bad quality ones. Because argument quality mostly matters for our opponents' arguments, our own thoughts have a massive advantage.

When I can't understand how someone can believe what they believe, I find it helpful to explicitly articulate little syllogisms from their perspective that start with the psychological bottom line premises. By the time I get to the end, their conclusion "therefore my preferred belief is true" makes a lot more sense.

Adopting this perspective means that we have to let go of the default theory we normally apply to human thinking. We implicitly assume that people process information like a computer. They are presented with new information, they compare it to their existing knowledge, weigh the plausibility of the evidence, and draw a conclusion. Reasoning in this view works in a straight line from premises to conclusions. That theory works for topics where our social identities are not involved. If I ask someone for directions, or read an article about how to grow hydrangeas, I don't have a predetermined conclusion in mind. So I take in the information and use it more or less according to the linear theory. I still generate cognitive responses and believe my own thoughts, but there is no reason that my own thoughts should disagree with what I'm being told.

Once identities are involved, and the psychological immune system goes to work, things play out very differently. We still take in information, compare it to existing knowledge, and weigh the evidence. But the game is rigged. We know the conclusion we want to reach, we generate the arguments we need to get us there, and then we believe those arguments. The new information rarely stands a chance. That's because once the psychological immune system is involved, reasoning operates not in a straight line but in circles. As soon as you reach a conclusion that conflicts with something else you want to believe, you go back and start again, trying some new arguments.

There is not a fundamentally different process for motivated reasoning versus "regular" reasoning. When we try to solve a brain teaser, the first line of reasoning might lead us astray. For example: "A Ferrari and a Ford together cost $190,000. The Ferrari costs $100,000 more than the Ford. How much does the Ford cost?" The first answer that comes to mind for most people is that the Ford costs $90,000. But that can't be right, because if the Ferrari costs $100,000 more than the Ford, then it costs $190,000 by itself. That would mean that together, they cost $280,000. So we go back to the drawing board and work through the problem again. After another loop or two, we figure out that the Ford must cost $45,000, so that the Ferrari costs $145,000, and together they add up to $190,000. We just keep working through the loops until everything fits together, or we get tired of the problem and move on to something more interesting.

Think about that tense, uneasy feeling we get when we realize that things are not adding up. Our eyes squint, as if focusing better will make things clear. We lean forward, as if looking more closely will help. Some people experience a slight headache or a pit in the stomach. In twentieth-century psychology, that feeling of inner conflict was called "cognitive dissonance." In modern neuroscience, it is called "conflict detection." Whatever term we use, the fascinating thing is that neurologically, the aversive feeling of a logical contradiction overlaps heavily with the feeling of pain in general. Because of that, the unpleasant signal that means "this cannot be logically correct" feels essentially the same as "if this is true, then my group and I are wrong." Both motivate us to keep thinking until we get a better solution.

The reasoning loops we go through are less like the linear thinking of a computer and more like painting. If something doesn't feel right, you can always go back and change it. News channels and social media are constantly serving up an assortment of arguments to fill your palette. If one combination doesn't work, you can keep mixing and shading until everything feels right.

Psychologists like to catalog cognitive biases, giving each one a unique name. We have the anchoring bias (getting stuck on an idea that we considered first), the availability bias (judging based on what information comes easily to mind), the confirmation bias (finding evidence to support beliefs we already hold), the status quo bias (thinking that the way things are is the way things should be), and even the bias blind spot (the inability to see our own biases). The list goes on and on. It is tempting to ask what specific biases are at work when people engage in wishful thinking. But that's not really a question that can be answered, because there is no one pathway that people follow to reach their preferred conclusions. Think of the conclusions that we need to reach as destinations we want to travel to. If one route is blocked, we will just take another.

So why do we even bother thinking up arguments and reasoning through contradictions at all? Why not simply admit that we are largely impervious to evidence and reason and cling to our opinions in peace? Research suggests that it is, in large part, to make ourselves look good and reasonable to other people. Not just any other people, but the people whose opinions we value. That is, people in our own groups.

Studies find, for example, that people are better at arguing with other people than at thinking for themselves. Ask people to judge whether simple syllogisms are valid—*If there is smoke, there is fire. There is no fire, so there is no smoke*—and they often struggle. But ask them to use a syllogism to persuade other people, and they do much better. Even young children can spot reasoning fallacies, but only in other people. Cognitive scientists Hugo Mercier and Dan Sperber have convincingly argued that reasoning has developed not simply to find truth but to win friends and influence people—that is, to increase our status in the groups we care about.

Think about how different this explanation is from the way we explain our own reasons. We might say we prefer this set of policies to that one. We might say that this politician is honest and competent but the other one is corrupt. We might even say the other side are fascists or socialists bent on destroying America. But these explanations all point outside ourselves at something in the world: people, policies, threats *out there*. Imagine how ridiculous it would sound if we explained our beliefs based not on our reasons but on the causes for our reasons. "Look, I know what I want to end up believing," we might say, "so I'm just gonna keep jiggering ideas around until they fit with my preferred conclusion." But we don't say that. When an adult plugs their ears with their fingers and says "I can't hear you!" they look like a childish fool. So instead, we rationalize away the arguments we don't want to hear by smiling, nodding, and stringing together articulate sentences. We get to the same destination, but we travel there with more style.

Research on the psychological immune system suggests that it works basically the same for liberals and conservatives, for Democrats and Republicans. It is a fundamental part of the way humans think. And yet, when minds like this are dropped into an environment divided by political groups, the same thought cycles lead to very different beliefs. In the next chapter we see how the psychological immune system collides with political ideologies.

THREE

IDEOLOGY WITHOUT IDEAS

There are no grown-ups. Everyone is winging it.

—PAMELA DRUCKERMAN

When I went to college, there was a handful of big questions that I wanted to learn the answers to. Questions like, How does the stock market work? Everyone in the 1990s seemed to be getting rich from stocks. At least, that's what it looked like on TV. But no one I knew invested in the stock market. The only investments I knew about personally were when relatives loaned one another money to save their failing businesses, or when Dad and some of his friends went in together to drill an oil well in a western Kentucky tobacco field. As far as I could see, investing just meant losing your money.

Another big question was what made some books, like the Edgar Allan Poe we read in class, "serious literature" while other books, like Stephen King novels, were merely "popular fiction"? When I asked my literature professors if this wasn't just a matter of taste and snobbishness, they would sigh. One professor told me that there is a difference between sentiment (authentic emotion) and sentimentality (cheap ploys to make readers feel emotion). Another said that great works stand the test of time. I suggested that anything that managed to get handed down lots of generations would probably come to be regarded as great, even if it stunk. With gentleness and patience, he suggested that I keep reading, and eventually I would understand. I kept reading, but I still don't understand.

The other big question I kept trying to figure out was what *liberal* and *conservative* meant exactly. The words were everywhere, in the newspapers and the TV news, so I assumed everyone knew what they meant, and I had somehow been left out. I had a general image of what conservatives looked like (old White bankers) and what liberals looked like (hippies). But I couldn't put into words what the ideas really meant. I looked up classes on political ideologies, but they were not what I was looking for. They were too technical and oddly specific. They had names like The Rise and Fall of Marxism in Post-Colonial Bora Bora.

I asked my psychology and philosophy professors questions after class, but it was hard to get a straight answer. "Well, they mean different things to different people," one professor said. Another sighed and gave me a list of books to read. The books were helpful, but it was clear that he did not want to talk about the subject anymore. Far from the "liberal indoctrination" that many people assume goes on in universities, my professors seemed afraid to discuss politics at all.

Years later, that reading list would come in handy a second time. George W. Bush was president. When I moved from St. Louis to Columbus, Ohio, for my first job as a professor, the movers commented that I had a lot of (heavy) books. On the St. Louis side of the move, the upholstery on my sofa had gotten torn, and the moving company agreed to send me a check for its repair. The Columbus mover noticed the stack of books my professor had recommended, and he was captivated. There were some people in his family, he said, who were going nuts about politics. They could not have a reasonable or civil conversation about any of it, and he was trying his best to understand why they believed the things they believed. So he proposed a deal. He happened to have a furniture upholstering business on the side. He would fix my couch for free. In return, I would give him a few of the books explaining political ideology and correspond with him for a while about other books he might read.

We corresponded over email for a couple of months, as he devoured books like Bob Altemeyer's *Right-Wing Authoritarianism* and Erich Fromm's *Escape from Freedom*. Like me, he was surrounded by a constant cacophony of talk about left and right, and he longed to make sense of all the noise. As we will see in this chapter, many Americans find themselves in the same position.

As I struggled to make sense of these questions, the people I knew during my college years who claimed to be liberal or conservative didn't clear things up. Dad described himself as "pretty conservative" but always voted for Democrats. Mom claimed to be middle of the road but voted mostly Republican. If my adult siblings voted at all, they never talked about it.

In college I hung around with artsy types, like the theater kids who would break out in show tunes in the middle of a conversation or flip into an impression of Carol Channing without warning. There was Stacia, who rebelled against her Catholic parents by dressing in bell bottoms and calling herself Wiccan. She still snuck off to Mass on Sundays. Then there was Sam, who dressed like the guys from Weezer, with a cardigan over a T-shirt with an ironic saying on it. Another circle of my friends were literary types. We would drink cheap wine until we got up the courage to read poetry at open mic nights. I grew my hair into long ringlets and wore baggy sweaters made of hemp.

We certainly looked the part of "leftist" college students. Except we never talked about politics. Bill Clinton was president, and we thought the Monica Lewinsky affair was hilarious. Sam took Economics 101 and got enamored with Friedrich Hayek. He started talking about the Laffer curve for a while. No one argued with him. We just shrugged and passed the joint. I thought everyone else must have understood the political landscape and were too cool to spend time on it. I assumed they figured out some philosophy of life, some code to live by, that I hadn't figured out. But looking back, I'm pretty sure they didn't understand political ideas any more than I did.

It wasn't until my final year of college and into graduate school that I started learning about the philosophical ideas behind liberalism and conservatism. I read early conservative thinkers like Edmund Burke in England and Joseph de Maistre in France, who laid out the basic philosophy that has guided conservative intellectual traditions for more than two centuries.

Conservative philosophy starts with a dim view of human nature. In the religious version, we are fallen from grace, carrying with us the burden of original sin. Or in more secular versions, we are simply selfish, shortsighted, and weak willed. Because of the depravity in human nature, you can expect the worst of people, unless they are restrained by strong forces of social order.

Two forces, in particular, are seen as necessary to restrain the constant threat of chaos. The first is tradition. Following the senseless destruction of the Thirty Years' War, European thinkers considered civilization and peace to be precious, hard won, and scarce. Tradition is the set of practices that has emerged over centuries as the best way to maintain stability. Even if we think there might be a better way to do something, human rationality is too fickle to be trusted. At the time these authors were writing, the Scientific Revolution was in full swing. Galileo had long ago shown that Earth moved around the sun and not the other way around, as the Catholic Church insisted. Newton showed that gravity was the universal force that kept the planets in orbit, and his three laws of motion had revolutionized all of physics. New, powerful telescopes allowed astronomer William Herschel to watch stars being born in far-off nebulae, while Antonie van Leeuwenhoek watched bacteria squirm beneath the lens of his microscope.

Edmund Burke was unimpressed. "In this enlightened age," Burke wrote, "I am bold enough to confess, that we are generally men of untaught feelings; that instead of casting away all our old prejudices, we cherish them." He went on to argue that the "prejudices" and "illusions" of tradition are socially necessary and better than expecting each person to make choices based on "his own private stock of reason."

The second stabilizing force was hierarchy. Burke argued that the secular authority of the aristocracy and the divine order of the Church were necessary to prevent chaos. Enlightenment ideas, Maistre argued, were responsible for the wave of disastrous revolutionary movements that were destabilizing Europe. Law and order, he argued, were necessary to restrain the lawlessness of human hearts. "All power, all subordination rests on the executioner," he said. "He is the horror and the bond of human association. Remove this incomprehensible agent from the world, and the very moment order gives way to chaos, thrones topple, and society disappears."

The emphasis on tradition and respect for hierarchy meant that the job of government was not to fix problems but to maintain social order. These writers were unconcerned about the plight of the peasants, who were dominated by the aristocrats, or the freethinkers, who were persecuted by the Church. The social order was more important than the individuals within it, and in a hierarchy some people always had to be on bottom while others were on top. Well-intentioned efforts to reform society for the benefit of the poor and powerless, they argued, risked turning into chaos. Burke's credibility rose sharply when his prediction that the French Revolution would descend into a bloody Reign of Terror came to pass.

Early liberal thinkers, on the other hand, were much more taken with the sense of progress that was sweeping the world. For writers like John Locke, oppressive institutions like monarchy and Church were part of the problem. More than a century of scientific progress had shown that human reason could do amazing things. So why not let people decide for themselves what path they want to take?

Liberalism starts with no particular philosophy of human nature. Locke famously assumed a blank slate, in which there is little or no human nature at all. Other versions assume that people do start out with different abilities and preferences, but those differences are irrelevant to the way society should be organized. What mattered for Locke is that we have natural, individual rights—rights to freedom of thought, freedom of speech, and freedom of religion. If exercising freedom of thought leads someone to question their religion or to criticize power structures, then so be it. After all, the government was not some divine authority but merely an expedient tool—a social contract—that individuals consented to because it was useful.

While Locke articulated the importance of individual rights, it was John Stuart Mill who, a generation later, sketched the shape of modern liberalism. He defended free speech and tolerance of heretical views not on the basis of natural rights, but because people are fallible. Hence, the best way to stumble gradually toward truth is to try persuading other people with your best arguments.

Mill was a utilitarian who argued that the moral good is not whatever is decreed by God or valued by tradition. It is whatever brings about the most happiness for the most people. We don't always know what will bring about the most happiness, so people should be free to tinker until we find something that works better. Mill's idea of "experiments in living" could not be further from Burke's emphasis on preserving tradition and the status quo.

Utilitarian ethics tend to be egalitarian, because hierarchies are shaped like pyramids—there are a few rulers at the top and many commoners at the bottom. So helping those at the bottom brings about a greater improvement of the common good. Not surprisingly, Mill was a proponent of equal rights for women and Black people, and he thought it was part of the government's job to secure those rights. It does a society no good, he argued, "to ordain that to be born a girl instead of a boy, any more than to be born black instead of white, or a commoner instead of a nobleman, shall decide the person's position through all of life."

There are countless variations on these ideological sketches, but I expect most readers will recognize them and resonate with one worldview or the other. Two centuries later, conservatives are not arguing for monarchy or aristocracy, but valuing traditional versions of social order at the expense of equality is familiar. For Christian conservatives, the authority of religion seems under siege and needs to be defended against the forces of individual choice. Aristocracy has given way to meritocracy, as conservatives see wealthy business owners as job creators and oppose raising taxes on the wealthy to help the poor, lest they become dependent on government help. Liberals no longer have to argue that slavery should be abolished or that women should be able to vote. But the indifference to tradition and the desire to use government to erode continuing forms of inequality still rings true. Social welfare programs and race-conscious college admissions are their modern tools. Liberals still find the root causes of society's problems in the very same places—tradition and hierarchy—that conservatives see the solutions.

In every generation, people look around and see both tradition and change. Conservatives look at the changing landscape and say, "That's far enough, that's too fast." Liberals look at the same landscape and say, "That's too little and too slow." Based on these fundamental differences, they adopt different views on policies. Conservatives favor traditional sources of morality, from Christianity to conventional family structures, to constrain human frailty. Doubting the power of individual reason, they gravitate toward "small government" rather than centrally planned solutions. They want the government to stay mostly out of economic life, with low taxes and little regulation of business. For conservatives, the less the government is involved, the more individuals are free to make their own way. Ronald Reagan captured this philosophy in his farewell address when he said, "Man is not free unless government is limited. There's a clear cause and effect here that is as neat and predictable as a law of physics: As government expands, liberty contracts."

Liberals, with their greater trust in individual reason, gravitate toward policies that reduce historical inequalities and solve problems. They support government regulation of businesses to prevent them from ruining the environment or taking advantage of customers. Skeptical that hierarchy is a legitimate result of equal opportunity, they want to tax the rich and redistribute money to help the poor. Sensitive to past and present racial discrimination, they support affirmative action policies to rebalance opportunities. John F. Kennedy encapsulated this philosophy when he said, "If by a 'Liberal' they mean . . . someone who looks ahead and not behind, someone who welcomes new ideas without rigid reactions, someone who cares about the welfare of the people—their health, their housing, their schools, their jobs, their civil rights, and their civil liberties—someone who believes we can break through the stalemate and suspicions that grip us in our policies abroad, if that is what they mean by a 'Liberal,' then I'm proud to say I'm a 'Liberal.'"

That, at least, is the way it works in theory. Notice that I have adopted here the familiar way of describing these differences as different types of people: conservatives think this, while liberals think that. This presumes that some people are conservatives, in the sense that they adopt a philosophical framework that is at least roughly in line with the ideas of people like Burke. And other people are liberals, who adopt a philosophy something like the ideas of Mill. However, social science research for the last sixty years has made clear again and again that the vast majority of people— including those who express strong political views—have virtually no political ideology. And so it makes no sense to call most people liberals or conservatives.

Wait, what? How can that possibly be? Isn't the country being torn apart by the divisions between liberals and conservatives? Isn't that what "polarization" is all about? Isn't that the very point of this book? Let me explain.

INNOCENT OF IDEOLOGY

By the 1960s, political scientists had become very, very good at doing survey research. They had perfected probability sampling, a statistical approach to ensure that the results of a survey reflected not just the opinions of the people surveyed but the larger population. As a result, they could make accurate conclusions (within a margin of error) about what the public believed. The first widely known poll to use this technique was by George Gallup in the 1936 presidential election. Others were already conducting polls, but using unscientific methods. *The Literary Digest*, for example, surveyed its readers and had correctly predicted the several previous elections. In 1936, they predicted that Alf Landon would defeat Franklin Roosevelt. Gallup disagreed. When Roosevelt was reelected in a landslide, the new statistical methods were vindicated. Gallup rose to prominence and *The Literary Digest*, its credibility diminished, folded soon after.

Armed with more reliable methods, polls and surveys became more widespread throughout the 1940s, '50s, and '60s. In 1948, the American National Election Studies were created. They not only used scientific sampling methods, but they measured the same opinions using the same questions year after year to measure how opinions changed over time. As researchers looked closely at survey responses, a disturbing portrait of the American voter began to emerge: They seemed to have no idea what they were talking about.

The argument was made in a 1964 essay by political scientist Philip Converse. Using several years of survey data, he looked at multiple measures of how people understood and used ideology. As a first pass, he looked at how well people understood what the terms *liberal* and *conservative* mean. The researchers scored them according to whether they correctly used ideas (in their own words) from liberal and conservative intellectual traditions—like status quo versus social change, large versus small government, individual rights versus traditional social order, or free enterprise versus the welfare state. Only 17 percent could correctly explain the terms. Thirty-seven percent could give no answer at all. The rest offered an answer, but it was either wrong or so vague or muddled as to be uninterpretable. Most people did not appear to understand the terms any better than I did as a college freshman.

Maybe the survey respondents had an ideology but were simply not very good at explaining it the way the researchers wanted. Real life, after all, is not a college seminar. To investigate this possibility, Converse looked at how respondents' opinions to various issues correlated with one another. An ideology is a coherent system of ideas. If people had a real ideology that fell along the liberal-conservative dimension, then their opinions toward logically related ideas should be correlated with one another. For example, people who think that taxes should be cut should also tend to think that benefits to the poor should be reduced. Those who support government aid for education ought to also support the government ensuring that fair housing policies are enforced. And people who support an interventionist foreign policy should also support high levels of funding for the military.

When Converse looked at the correlations between related issues for the general public, they were almost entirely absent. Whether people took the liberal or conservative side on one issue said almost nothing about whether they took the liberal or conservative position on other issues, even issues that were logically connected. When people expressed their opinions on a range of political issues, they did not show up as liberals or conservatives. It was as if they were responding mostly at random.

Still, it is possible that people have coherent ideologies, but they don't line up neatly along the liberal-conservative continuum. Maybe each person has their own constellation of principles and issue stands based on their personal philosophy? One person might be conservative on economic issues, for example, but liberal on social issues, or vice versa. Another might have hawkish views on foreign policy but be moderate on issues of domestic politics. Such heterodox philosophies would look like a lack of ideology in Converse's analyses, when in fact they could be sophisticated ideologies.

There is a genre of sober political analysis that endlessly tries to dissect what voters really believe and what they want based on election results. When George W. Bush was president, analysts concluded that the typical voter must prefer the "compassionate conservatism" of immigration reform paired with a hawkish foreign policy. When Barack Obama was elected, analysts concluded that people wanted hope, change, and an end to the bitter partisanship of the previous eight years. And when Donald Trump was elected, those same analysts concluded that the people were tired of moderation on immigration and wanted a combative response to elites. These portraits of the electorate, of course, are just the politicians' main talking points. These sophisticated blends of libertarianism, nationalism, and communitarianism (all the isms!) exist in lots of think tank white papers. But do real voters actually have such nuanced ideologies?

To answer this question, Converse looked at how stable people's views were over time. If each person operates according to their own personal code, those codes should at least be consistent over time. And yet, they were not. Someone who wanted tax increases during an election year might support tax cuts by the midterms. A person who thought the government should do more to protect racial minorities on one survey would think it should do less at the next survey. Even opinions about lightning-rod issues like abortion showed little stability over time.

How inconsistent were people? If they closed their eyes and pulled "agree" and "disagree" responses from a hat, they would agree with themselves 50 percent of the time by chance alone. In their responses to surveys about real political opinions, they agreed with themselves only about 65 percent of the time. That's slightly better than chance, but far from what we would expect of people whose opinions are guided by a coherent ideology.

Converse identified a few exceptions to this general lack of ideology. Politicians themselves had clear ideologies. They tended to be reliably liberal or conservative, and they were consistent in their views over time. Other "elites" such as journalists and academics whose fields relate to politics also showed evidence of genuine ideologies. And a minority of ordinary people who scored highly on a test of political knowledge showed a fair degree of coherence. But these groups make up a very small segment of the public. Converse estimated that around 15 percent of the population could be considered to have a political ideology. The other 85 percent, he concluded, were "innocent of ideology."

Converse's study was done in the 1960s, when politics in America was much less polarized than today. The Democratic Party was an alliance between two factions. Southern Democrats dominated the South and stood, above all, for preserving the Jim Crow system of racial segregation as part of the southern "way of life." In the North, Democrats were the union-friendly party of primarily working-class Whites. The Republican Party was the party of big business. There were conservative Republicans, like Barry Goldwater, and liberal Republicans, like Nelson Rockefeller. Black Americans and many immigrant groups were still largely left out in the early 1960s.

The upshot of these party cleavages was that there was no clear match between political parties and liberal versus conservative ideologies. Given how little polarization there was in the '60s, it is no wonder Converse found little evidence for ideological divides among the public. Surely, if the same study were done today, things would be radically different. Democrats would express consistently liberal views and Republicans consistently conservative ones. That, at least, is the intuition that many analysts have had over the past forty years. Then political scientists Nathan Kalmoe and Donald Kinder put that idea to the test.

They updated Converse's analyses using current survey data. What they found shocked many readers. Like Converse, they found that few Americans could correctly define what *liberal* or *conservative* means. And like Converse, they found that knowing whether a person had a liberal or conservative view on one issue provided very little information about which view they would take on other related issues. When they followed people over time, they found that people's political opinions were no more stable than in 1964.

The same exceptions applied. Politicians, journalists, and academics appeared to have ideologies, but the vast majority of Americans showed no evidence of having one.

There was one other exception that was present both in Converse's original study and in Kalmoe and Kinder's later version. It is an exception that makes both these studies make more sense in light of the fiery political conflicts we see today. Although most people are wildly inconsistent when it comes to political issues like taxes, government spending, and so on, they are highly coherent when it comes to their social groups. Partisanship, in particular, was highly stable. If a person rates themselves as a strong Democrat or a strong Republican today, they will likely identify with the same party a few years from now. And if they really hated the other party, they would likely still hate the party later.

The other set of opinions that showed this kind of stability was racial attitudes. When respondents were asked about whether racism is a thing of the past, or whether Black people have too much influence in politics, or even how warm or cold they felt toward different racial groups, their answers were stable and coherent.

The picture of voters emerging from this research is one that political scientists, political strategists, and politicians themselves have understood for a long time but that everyday discussions of politics always seem to get wrong. Most people have no ideology, if an ideology is understood as a coherent set of principles, or even a coherent set of issue opinions. What they have, instead, is group loyalties and the desire for their groups to dominate other groups. And as we saw in chapter 2, once people identify as part of a group, their psychological immune systems kick in to ensure that no matter what happens, they can see themselves and their groups as good and reasonable people.

Today, according to Pew research, about 31 percent of American adults call themselves Democrats, and 26 percent identify as Republicans. The remaining 38 percent call themselves Independents. But in reality, about 80 percent of Independents consistently side with one party or the other; they just don't want to be labeled as such. So the more realistic numbers are 48 percent Democrats and 39 percent Republicans. Only about 7 percent of Americans are truly independent in the sense that they don't lean consistently toward either party. Those independents are even less knowledgeable and less politically engaged than the general population. Almost everybody has a social identity on the line, even when they don't have clear ideas about political issues.

THE ILLUSION OF IDEOLOGY

Political issues are only weakly tied to these deeper group loyalties. They are tools that people pick up and lay down, as needed, to justify their group status. That is why they are so inconsistent. It's not that people are unintelligent. Politics is simply too abstract and distant for most people to invest a lot of time and effort to understanding it in detail. Baseball fans have detailed, specific, and coherent beliefs about baseball, and classical music aficionados have coherent sets of beliefs about classical music. But imagine what would happen if we polled a sample of ordinary Americans about classical music, simply assuming that they had knowledge and opinions about it. A standard survey question might read: "Would you say music from the Romantic period is more emotionally powerful or less emotionally powerful than music from the Baroque period?" And then respondents would indicate their answer on a 5-point scale from "Romantic period is much more emotionally powerful" to "Baroque period is much more emotionally powerful." The vast majority of respondents would answer the question the best they can, but their answers wouldn't mean anything.

Some people are classical music devotees, some are baseball fans, and some are political junkies. But most people are not. So when it comes to political issue opinions, most people are winging it—just making things up as they go along. People rarely even remember what their opinion was on charter schools or climate policy a year ago. If you survey them a year later, they will make it up as they go based on whatever cues are easily available at the moment, just as they did the first time.

My research, with psychologist Jazmin Brown-Iannuzzi and other colleagues, suggests that people's political views can shift dramatically even from one moment to another, when their place in a hierarchy changes. In some of our research, for example, we asked participants to research and pick stocks to see who could make the most profitable investments based on a simulation of the real stock market. The participants took their task seriously, reading about the companies and weighing their options. Some focused on the price-to-earnings ratio. Others considered the industry each company was in, and whether conditions were favorable for that kind of business in the current economy. Some picked stocks that were on an upward trajectory, while others chose the stocks that had recently dipped, hoping to catch a good value when the stock price rose again.

None of this careful research mattered, because in reality we randomly assigned participants to be winners or losers in our experiment. Everyone "earned" the exact same amount of money, but we told the winners that they had done better than most other participants, and we told the losers that they had fared worse than most. Because of this random assignment, we know the winners were not actually any more competent than the losers, and the two groups did not differ in personalities or values or background, on average. So by comparing the two groups we could test the effect of simply experiencing the circumstance of being higher or lower status.

When we asked them to explain why they performed the way they did, the losers justified their failure by claiming the game was unfair. The winners, on the other hand, justified their success by attributing it to skill, intelligence, and hard work. They rated the losers as less intelligent and less hardworking.

To understand what this means for political views, we asked participants in our study some more questions about income taxes and the social safety net. The losers said we should raise taxes on the wealthy and strengthen the social safety net. But the winners, confident in the meritocracy that allowed them to excel, said we should lower taxes on the wealthy and cut benefits to the poor. When we showed each group the opinions of the other group, they thought the other group was biased, incompetent, and blinded by self-interest.

The first reaction many people have when I describe this study is to say, "Look at those hypocrites! The losing team is just saying the game was unfair out of a sour-grapes attempt to rationalize their failure. And the winners are smugly taking credit for good fortune they didn't earn. They are born on third base and think they hit a triple." But if that is all you see, then you have missed the point. Think about what it is like to be in the position of these participants. They have invested time and effort in studying the stocks and making their decisions. More important, they know deep down that they are good, smart, and reasonable people. They have known it all their lives, just as surely as the rest of us know it about ourselves.

If you are told that you did worse than most other participants, what seems like the most reasonable explanation? One reaction is to think, *Maybe I'm not very good at picking stocks. Maybe I'm not even very good at making intelligent decisions in general.* That conclusion would feel bad, of course. But it would also open up all kinds of other self-doubts. *Does this mean that I need to rethink other important decisions I've made? Will I be able to make good choices for my retirement account?*

Another reaction is to think it's a silly game anyway and probably rigged. So the stock-picking game says nothing about me as a person. Starting with the premise that I am a good, smart, and reasonable person, the dismissive reaction seems much more plausible. And in fact, this is the reaction that most participants in the losing condition had.

Now consider what things look like from the winners' point of view. One could take the same dismissive approach as the losers took, decide that the game was meaningless and take no real pride in being a winner in this silly game. Or, again starting from the premise that I am a good, smart, and reasonable person, I could lean into the message that I really am a winner. *I mean, I did put in a lot of effort reading and thinking about those P/E ratios. Maybe this means I am unusually skilled at picking stocks. After all, I've always known I was smarter than average.*

When people start from the assumption that they are good and smart and reasonable, there is nothing illogical about evaluating new information in ways that are consistent with that assumption. In fact, considering starting assumptions—what statisticians call base rates—is actually a logically savvy thing to do when drawing inferences from data. And when they do that, they will tend to behave just like the subjects in our experiment: The winners will conclude that they earned their success through skill and hard work. The losers, meanwhile, will conclude that they were the victims of a rigged game.

From the outside, we can see that this is a self-serving bias. But we all have self-serving biases. The challenge in understanding the meaning of studies like this is to hold two ideas in mind at the same time. First, people start with the assumption that they are good and smart and reasonable people, and therefore will have all sorts of self-serving biases. And second, they are actually being smart and reasonable people from the only point of view they have, looking out through their own eyes, just like you and I are.

This study is a microcosm of our political divisions. People find themselves in one place or another in a social hierarchy, and they try to make sense of it. Their psychological immune systems spin different stories at the top or the bottom, helping participants in both groups feel that they are good and competent people in a world that makes sense.

Being randomly assigned to one condition or another in an experiment is like a roll of the dice. Chance places us in one set of circumstances or another. In ordinary life, chance plays a far more powerful role than many of us recognize. We are born to wealth or poverty. We are born in bodies with light or dark skin. Into a family of some particular religion or perhaps none at all. In a small town or a big city, in a place with a vast shadowy expanse of history that was playing out long before our individual light winked into existence and that will go on long after we have returned to the shadows. In the brief interval in between, we work hard to make sense of it all.

In 2008, then candidate Barack Obama made a gaffe when he said of people in midwestern industrial towns that had been decimated by job losses that they "cling to guns or religion or antipathy to people who aren't like them or anti-immigrant sentiment or anti-trade sentiment as a way to explain their frustrations." When the remarks were made public, he was criticized as being elitist and dismissive of voters' concerns. He eventually apologized. But psychologically speaking, he was right. People do adopt political beliefs to make sense of why they feel the way they feel and why they are in the position they are in. Mr. Obama was talking about why many Rust-Belt Americans sometimes favor Republicans. But the same kind of remark could be made about why many vote Democrat (formerly industrial cities in the Midwest are about evenly politically divided). An uncharitable critic might say that they cling to their "woke" ideas about equality and inclusiveness and their antipathy toward police as ways to explain their frustrations about inequality.

A more charitable and, more important, more psychologically accurate description is to say that both groups use political ideas as tools for their psychological immune systems. But as Converse showed, they don't create a coherent, consistent set of ideas. They just spin stories on the fly. This is not to say they are being dishonest. To the contrary, the psychological immune system works only if you sincerely believe the story you are telling. The best way to view the rationalizations people use is to assume that they really believe what they are saying—in the moment—while also understanding that they may believe something completely different next week.

All of this sensemaking and psychological immune defense creates an illusion of ideology. Consider a series of curious experiments led by psychologists Lars Hall and Petter Johansson. They gave participants a paper-and-pencil survey about a range of political topics. Examples included whether a wealth tax should be implemented and whether the government should be allowed to monitor citizens' phone traffic to protect against terrorism. After each participant completed the survey, the experimenters used a magician's sleight of hand to change the answers on a few questions and then gave the survey back. Then they asked participants to explain why they answered the way they did. Participants only noticed the switch on 22 percent of the questions. Astonishingly, on the majority of switched questions, participants then proceeded to explain why they chose an answer that they had in fact rejected. And the explanations they gave were every bit as sincere and compelling as the explanations they gave to answers that they actually had chosen.

These experiments have been repeated in Sweden, Argentina, and the United States, and the results are fairly consistent. At least half of the time, people fail to notice the switch and rattle off reasonable-sounding explanations for their political opinions whether they existed a moment ago or not. In real life, of course, magicians do not go around switching the opinions you just expressed. But these experiments are remarkable for the insight they provide about how humans actually think.

These results make no sense if you think of humans as ideological thinkers who start with political principles and then apply them to particular issue opinions. But the results make perfect sense if you instead start with Converse's view of ordinary people as "innocent of ideology." They have little ideological content to begin with, but a clear sense of which team they are on. From there, they improvise something to say that sounds reasonable in the moment based on whatever cues are noticeable in the immediate surroundings.

People are pretty good at this improvisation. In everyday life, the cues most available to people are talking points from their own team—news stories, political leaders, or talking heads from their side of the aisle who are easy to call to mind. And so the typical Republican ends up expressing views that sound a lot like Fox News and the typical Democrat sounds a lot like *The New York*

Times. If you have a conversation with someone about politics they will usually say things that sound like they have well-thought-out opinions. They talk about taxes or police reform or welfare benefits. But unless they are a small minority of elites and political experts, what they are really saying, like baseball fans on a train platform, is: "The other side sucks!"

In the moment, it's hard to believe that there's no one home. It is only under the strange conditions of an experiment, where the immediate cues have been switched, that we can see that people are largely making it up as they go. Viewing political arguments this way, in my experience, is illuminating. Arguing about politics is frustrating because the person on the other side changes the topic, shifts the goalposts, and refuses to engage with the facts and reasoning that we have brought to bear. In those moments, it is helpful to pause and realize that there may be no coherent belief system there, and that this person is simply winging it. They are trying to come up with arguments that will preserve the bottom line that they are good and reasonable and their group is good and reasonable.

When someone espouses a view that seems inconsistent with logic and evidence, our immediate reaction is usually to think, "How can they believe that?" But a better question is, "What function is this belief serving for them at this moment?" Viewing people this way takes practice. It is even harder to realize that we may be doing the same thing ourselves.

This chapter has been an extended argument that what looks like differences in entrenched ideologies is not really about ideology for most people. The picture emerging of the ordinary voter is one who does not know or care much about politics and does not have a clear-cut set of ideological principles. When it comes to political issues, people are inconsistent in their logic and unstable over time. That is why debating political ideas with other people can be so frustrating. We assume that if we could just get them to understand the facts, they would change their minds. The reality, though, is that people do not vote the way they vote because of what they believe. They believe what they believe because of how they want to vote.

Those votes are based on group identities. How do those identities arise? We rarely choose them for ourselves. They are thrust upon us by accidents of history. Imagine what would happen if you took a human mind, equipped with a powerful psychological immune system, and you dropped it into different times and places throughout history. Drop it into a citizen of ancient Rome, for example, and it will start defending the superiority of Roman civilization. Drop it into a first-century Christian, and it will argue that their persecution by the Romans is brutal and unjust. So why do some social groups come to define our identities, while others don't? To begin answering those questions, the next chapter zooms out to look at the way history sets us on different paths. The answers are buried even deeper than you think.

FOUR

LINCOLN'S MAP

They are just what we would be in their situation.

—ABRAHAM LINCOLN

L ong before there was a Mason-Dixon Line, there was an ancient coastline. A hundred million years ago, the Appalachian Mountains sloped down to the warm sea that covered most of the southern states. The water wrapped around the coastline, encroaching first where Maryland meets Pennsylvania. It covered the Chesapeake Bay and most of the Carolinas, cutting a swath through Georgia and Alabama, almost completely submerging Mississippi, Louisiana, and Texas. That coastline was a cosmic coin flip. It changed everything for the humans who would, much later, live on one side of it or the other.

The continents were still close in those days. The east coast of the Americas looked like a jigsaw puzzle piece that could fit snugly into the coastline of Africa. It still does, if you look carefully. Pangea, the supercontinent, was not too distant a memory.

On the land, it was the heyday of the dinosaurs. The big famous ones like _Tyrannosaurus rex_, _Triceratops_, and _Ankylosaurus_ with its tanklike armor. The water, too, was ruled by giants. There were turtles the size of trucks, carnivorous fish the size of canoes, and *Tylosaurus*, sea monsters as long as a school bus. As powerful as these giants were, our lives have been shaped even more profoundly by the tiniest of creatures floating all around them.

Microscopic plankton, each one with a shell of calcium, called coccoliths, floated in the ocean by the trillions. Some looked like tiny spheres made of sand dollars. Others looked like delicate ceramic statues of flowers. One by one, as each little creature died and floated to the sea floor, its crystalline shell added imperceptibly to the layer of chalk at the bottom of the sea. The chalk layer grew by half a millimeter per year, year after year, century after century, millennium after millennium. Over eons too great to comprehend, it came to cover nearly everything. This archeological period—the Cretaceous period—is Latin for the "time of chalk." The chalk, a type of limestone, lay there underwater as the asteroid struck and volcanoes erupted and the skies burned. The dinosaurs all died, the waters receded, and the continents continued drifting quietly apart.

The chalk is still there. When you write with a piece of old-fashioned chalk on a blackboard, the white dust flaking off is those ancient shells. In England it created the gleaming White Cliffs of Dover. They form a sheer drop in most places, from grassy fields down to the English Channel, separating England from France. During the Second World War, the cliffs were the last glimpse of home that many soldiers saw as they left for the front and the first familiar sight welcoming the ones who made it home.

On our side of the pond the chalky limestone remained mostly underground, peeking out here and there where springs bubbled up from the earth below. The bright white rocks glinting in streams caught the eyes of settlers, who gave their settlements names like Chalk, Texas, and Limestone County, Alabama. The chalk also formed a stark boundary that is still with us. But the border is no longer in the land so much as in our minds. Today, the amount of chalk in the soil can predict how residents vote, how they worship, and how they see the world. Many of the political, social, and moral divides that separate us today can be traced to the chalky residue of that long-gone ocean. The thread that connects that ancient past to our lives today is made of cotton.

THE COTTON THREAD

Cotton is an unforgiving plant. It needs long hot growing seasons, and it can't handle acidic soil. Chemically speaking, limestone is a base—it neutralizes acid. Add that to the hot southern climate, and you have two reasons that the southeastern United States became one of the best places on the planet to grow cotton. Almost no one was growing it at the time of the American Revolution. But cotton farming spread gradually through the early 1800s and then rapidly in midcentury. By 1860, the American South produced two thirds of the world's cotton. Most of the cotton was exported to England, where it was woven into textiles. But this was no ordinary trade. This system, in which cotton was grown in the southern states and processed in English factories, utterly changed the world. It fueled one of the biggest advances that ever happened: the Industrial Revolution. And one of the worst catastrophes that ever happened: chattel slavery.

In England, spinning and weaving required some skill, but these tasks were also highly repetitive. This kind of work can easily be automated. But to be automated, someone first had to invent the machines. Cotton factories provided the laboratories of invention. The spinning jenny spun raw cotton into threads many times faster than a person could by hand. The flying shuttle wove threads into cloth at speeds the previous generation could not have imagined. At first these machines were powered by waterwheels. But by 1776, James Watt and Matthew Boulton had developed a steam engine that could power whole factories. The cotton trade not only made American planters and English factory owners rich, it helped to spark the invention of mechanized manufacturing itself. The inventions created in places like Liverpool and Manchester would soon transform the world economy, lifting millions of people out of poverty.

Meanwhile, in the United States, southern planters were becoming fabulously wealthy by expanding cotton growing. It started near the coast, in Virginia and the Carolinas, and spread west and south, following the path of chalk. The planters didn't know that's what they were doing. They just kept expanding the profitable crop wherever it could thrive. If they planted it too far north or at too high an altitude, the cotton plant didn't grow. But in the places that had been submerged beneath the ocean so long ago, cotton grew fast and filled acre after acre with long, straight rows of lopsided white puffs.

Wherever cotton expanded, slavery did too. Cotton is a labor-intensive plant, and southern planters were willing and able to exploit the forced labor of enslaved people to grow it. As a result, they outcompeted other areas of the world where cotton was grown and became the world's leading producer.

Slavery had been a part of the English colonies from the beginning. The first documented slave ship arriving in the colonies was the *White Lion*, which came to port in Jamestown in 1619. It was a privateer ship—a privately owned vessel that was commissioned by a government to engage in warfare. Pirates with papers, they were called. The *White Lion* kidnapped around sixty enslaved men, women, and children from a Portuguese ship and brought them to Jamestown. The Portuguese crew had kidnapped them in present-day Angola. But this documented vessel wasn't the first slave ship to arrive—far from it. The fact that this was the first ship to be documented is an accident of history, due to the fact that the secretary of the colony happened to record the governor's purchase of the enslaved people in a letter. The remarkable thing, from our present perspective, is that slavery was so unremarkable that these transactions went largely unmentioned. Historians studying how people justified slavery noticed that nobody really bothered to justify it during colonial times. There were hardly any newspaper editorials or sermons either defending or criticizing the practice. It just did not seem to rate arguing over.

When the colonists started agitating for independence from Britain, things began to change. To justify their demands, they appealed to ideas from Enlightenment philosophy like natural rights. John Locke's ideas about the rights to "life, liberty, and property" became, in Thomas Jefferson's pen, the rights to life, liberty, and the pursuit of happiness. When he wrote that all men are created equal, what he had in mind was that the colonists were equal to Englishmen, and they were not going to be pushed around by Parliament without a seat at the table. But once the idea became popular, it took on a life of its own. It became impossible not to notice the contradiction between talk of equality and natural rights on the one hand and the practice of slavery on the other.

Some of the founding fathers, including Jefferson himself,

seemed to agonize about the contradiction. He opposed slavery in principle but argued that there was no feasible alternative. If slavery was abolished, he said, the result would be a race war. Whites would inevitably win, and the act would amount to a massacre of Black people. So slavery was not ideal, their reasoning went, but it was better for Black people than annihilation. At one point, Jefferson came up with a scheme to take enslaved children away from their parents to educate them and then send them to a new colony somewhere far away from White people. It did not occur to him that White people should change. Or that Whites could be educated in order to live peacefully together. So he wrote about natural rights while continuing to own slaves. But the cognitive dissonance went well beyond individual founders.

The uneasy tension between natural rights and slavery stirred some of the earliest abolitionist thinking around that time. And those abolitionist criticisms in turn provoked the early justifications of slavery. Curiously, the most common themes were the same ones that came up in Jefferson's defense. We didn't invent slavery, the justifiers would say, we just inherited it. Now that we've inherited it, we are stuck with it. It wasn't the current generation's fault, so they should not be held responsible for what previous generations did. So the best thing for everyone, they said, was just to keep the status quo.

You can almost see their psychological immune systems at work, trying to fit together their support of slavery with the assurance that they are good and reasonable people. In later years, especially in the southern states, the argument would expand to assert that slavery is actually good for slaves, because they would not be competent to take care of themselves if freed. But during the revolutionary years the main argument of the justifiers, in both the

North and the South, was that the only two alternatives were slavery or race war.

So in the years leading up to the Revolution, the abolitionists argued against slavery based on natural rights, while the establishment justified slavery. The abolitionists won debate after debate. First Vermont abolished slavery in 1777, followed by Pennsylvania, New Hampshire, and Massachusetts. In many of the states, actual emancipation was gradual, with newborn children considered free, while their parents remained enslaved. Still, the abolitionists were winning, and slave states were falling like dominoes and becoming free states. Slavery continued to fall through the early 1800s until it hit an unmovable boundary line. The line was made of chalk.

History has come to know the line separating North and South as the Mason-Dixon Line, after the English surveyors Charles Mason and Jeremiah Dixon, who were called in to settle a land dispute in 1765. King Charles I had given some land to Lord Baltimore, which he named Maryland after the king's wife, Queen Henrietta Maria. Fifty years later, Charles II gave some land to the Penn family, who named it after themselves. The boundary was drawn by local surveyors, but it was ragged and uneven. The messy lines left uncertainty as to who owned which land, and whether landowners owed taxes to Maryland or to Pennsylvania. Violence regularly erupted along the border, so pressure grew to settle the issue.

After years of quarreling over the boundary, the two families called in Mason and Dixon to survey the land and settle the boundary once and for all. Mason was a young genius, who was hired by the Royal Observatory at age twenty-eight and soon became a member of the Royal Society. Dixon also worked at the Royal Observatory and was a master astronomer. He was a Quaker, but not a very good one. He was excommunicated for drinking and carousing with women. Unlike the local surveyors, Mason and Dixon mapped the land the way they mapped the skies, using the stars to guide them. It was the most exact mapping that had ever been done in the New World.

They had no intention of drawing a line separating the North and the South. It just happened that the area where they split Maryland from Pennsylvania also generally lined up with the ancient coastline that covered the South in microscopic shells. What really split the North from the South then was the fact that cotton was so much more profitable in the chalky southern soil than in the North. In the North, enslavers were conflicted between the economic self-interest of keeping their slaves and the moral force of Enlightenment ideas. Enslavers felt the same conflict in the South, too, but the economic advantage was incomparably more powerful than in the North. The economic boom, driven by cotton, meant that the Enlightenment was simply overmatched in cotton-growing areas.

The chalk line set people on different paths. For those born north of it, Enlightenment ideas would ultimately seem more persuasive. For those born south of it, the economic benefits of slavery would be a more powerful force. There wasn't anything intrinsically different about northerners and southerners. They shared the same history, culture, and language. They read the same books and worshipped the same God. The difference was not something about the personalities or moral compasses of the people but the conditions they were living in.

Abraham Lincoln remarked on this in 1858, during one of his debates against Stephen Douglas in their contest for the Senate. Lincoln saw, more objectively than most, that human nature bends to self-serving biases. "They are just what we would be in their situation," he said of the southerners. "If slavery did not now exist amongst them, they would not introduce it. If it did now exist amongst us, we should not instantly give it up. This I believe of the masses north and south."

With the benefit of hindsight, we can see that Lincoln was right. But think of how different this view was from how ordinary people at the time thought about the conflict that was about to tear the country apart. Northerners could see slavery for the evil that it was, and they attributed that evil to the hearts of the southerners. There was not much conflict for their psychological immune systems to rationalize away. Southerners, on the other hand, rationalized that slavery wasn't evil at all, and the war, when it came, wasn't really about slavery anyhow. It was about the principle of states' rights (never mind what the states would do with those rights). After all, the Northern elites were being tyrants, trying to impose their stifling notions of moral superiority.

Each side was protecting its psychological bottom line that they and their groups were good and reasonable people, and they were doing it in predictable ways.

As a good politician, Lincoln was able to see the conflict brewing between North and South on two levels at once. First was the perspective of ordinary citizens who belonged to one group or the other and saw things only from their own side's point of view. But he also saw the role of history, economics, and geography that shaped those points of view. Like Lincoln, good social science also looks at human affairs from both levels at once. It understands the conflicts, dramas, outrages, and thrills that group members experience, while also understanding why anyone in that circumstance might share those same experiences.

Lincoln lost his Senate race, but two years later he won the presidency without carrying a single southern state. It was the final straw for many southerners. Although Lincoln did not campaign on a promise to abolish slavery, he was opposed to its expansion into Kansas, Nebraska, and the growing western territories. Slavery had been abolished in the North, and the transatlantic slave trade had been abolished by Britain in 1807 and then the United States in 1808. No new enslaved people were being brought to the U.S., and the South was surrounded by free territory. It was widely assumed that slavery would either expand into the West or it would die out, devastating the southern economy. Once Lincoln won, it was clear that he would stop slavery's western expansion. So the eleven states that formed the Confederacy began seceding. The North and the South prepared for war.

LINCOLN'S SLAVE MAP

One of President Lincoln's valuable tools in planning for the war was a special map created by the Coast Guard. Today the map sits in the Library of Congress, yellowed and brittle with age. Lincoln leaned over it, brooded over it, and kept it with him constantly as he strategized for the war. There is a famous painting of Lincoln and his cabinet when the president first unveils the Emancipation Proclamation. In the corner, you can see the map.

The reason Lincoln kept it by his side was that he knew that slavery was the key to the rebellion. The map used data from the 1860 census to show the percent of the population in each county that was enslaved. You can see the map in Figure 1. The darker the shading, the larger the proportion of the population that was enslaved. The darkest-shaded counties had populations that were around 90 percent enslaved. Displaying data on a map like this was new at the time, and it provided a powerful new weapon as the country hurtled toward war. Lincoln knew that the states most economically dependent on slavery would be the most committed to secession.

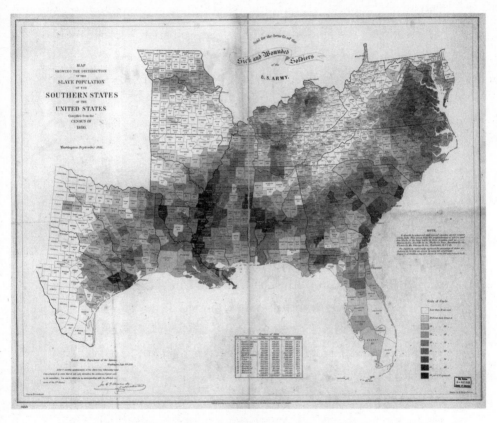

Figure 1.
Map showing the distribution of the slave population of the
southern states of the United States. Compiled from the census of 1860.
Ella Hergesheimer (Washington, D.C.: Henry S. Graham, 1861).
Library of Congress, Geography and Map Division.

The border states of Kentucky, Missouri, Delaware, and Maryland were critical to the war strategy. The million-dollar question was whether they would side with the Union or the Confederacy.

They had important railroads, natural resources, and a large combined population that would be a huge advantage to whichever army enlisted them. The border states all had slaves, but fewer than the states to their south, so Lincoln considered them persuadable. He did everything in his power to keep them as part of the Union. He removed secessionist state leaders and replaced them with loyalists. When he signed the Emancipation Proclamation, the border states were exempted so as not to alienate the slaveholders. He even approved a deal to carve West Virginia from Virginia. The mountainous terrain of West Virginia made the area poor land for cotton growing and meant they had few slaves and so were more sympathetic to the Union.

Sure enough, after Lincoln was elected, the states began seceding according to their enslaved populations. First South Carolina (57 percent enslaved) and then Mississippi (55 percent enslaved) left the Union. They were followed by Florida (44 percent), Alabama (45 percent), and Georgia (44 percent). One after another, the states seceded, until the eleventh and final Confederate state, Tennessee (25 percent), left the Union. Lincoln was right about the border states. Kentucky (20 percent), Maryland (13 percent), Missouri (10 percent), and Delaware (2 percent) did not join the Confederacy.

So the pattern of secession followed slavery. Slavery followed the location of the cotton. And the cotton followed the chalk. Those microscopic seashells, the cotton they grew, and the slavery the cotton enabled are still shaping our lives and our politics today. I don't mean in some abstract, metaphorical way like an "original sin," as some have argued. I mean in a concrete, literal way. The way that, the closer you grew up to Atlanta, the home of Coca-Cola, the more likely you are to call any soft drink a coke. The history of slavery and its aftermath set up the circumstances in which we now live in a thousand ways, some dramatic and some mundane. We don't reflect on these things and make a decision. If someone asked why you believed this idea and not that one, explaining about the geology of chalk would sound strange, at best. These are not reasons; they are the causes of our reasons.

Although the Civil War brought an end to slavery in the United States, the struggle over how free Black people and White people would live together had just begun. Although the war was over, the Reconstruction era was brutal in its own right. The northern public was weary of war and wanted its troops to return home. They wanted life to simply get back to normal. The South settled in for a long-term resistance campaign, determined to preserve as much of its racial order as it could. Having spent so many years justifying why the southern slave-based social order was right and just, losing the war was not enough to convince them otherwise. When people are convinced that they are good, reasonable people, losing to one's enemies is seen as a moral outrage.

On April 11, 1865, just two days after the Confederate surrender at Appomattox, Abraham Lincoln gave his last speech. He held up Louisiana as an example of how reconstruction could be carried out successfully. The state had established a pro-Union government and had set up schools for newly freed Black children. Their new state constitution outlawed slavery, and the state supported the Thirteenth Amendment, which banned slavery throughout the country. Although Louisiana had not allowed Black people to vote, Lincoln expressed the opinion that Black suffrage should be conferred on "the very intelligent, and on those who serve our cause as soldiers."

In the audience was John Wilkes Booth. He was so enraged at

the idea of Black citizenship and suffrage that he resolved then to murder the president, which he did three days later. Growing up and learning about the assassination of Abraham Lincoln, I was always puzzled why it had happened after the war was over. Wouldn't it have made more sense to assassinate a leader while it might still change the outcome of the war?

The answer has two parts. First, several attempts on his life actually were made throughout the war. Some of them were foiled, as when the newly elected Lincoln traveled from Illinois to Washington, D.C., secretly to avoid a plot against his expected train. Others failed through dumb luck, as when Lincoln returned from a solo horse ride to discover a bullet hole in his stovepipe hat.

The second part of the answer is that some southerners and southern sympathizers, like Booth, were more infuriated by the prospect of political and social equality for Black Americans than by the defeat of the Confederacy itself. Many southern Whites could reconcile themselves to being part of the Union. They could even resign themselves to the abolition of slavery. But they could not accept Black people having equal power.

Preserving the racial hierarchy became the main goal for southern legislatures. Once Andrew Johnson became president, southern states' ability to preserve the racial order was caught in the struggle between Johnson and Congress. Johnson, a southern Democrat, believed in abolition but did not believe that Black Americans could be politically or socially equal to Whites. He wanted the southern states reconciled to the Union as quickly as possible. Congress, controlled by Republicans, wanted to reconstruct the South as a multiracial democracy. The Freedmen's Bureau was set up to help newly freed people get an education and acquire land to farm for themselves. As a start, General William Tecumseh

Sherman ordered that four hundred thousand acres along the east coast of Georgia be confiscated from plantation owners and given to freedmen in plots of forty acres each. But Andrew Johnson overturned that order within the year and the new Black farmers were forced to hand the land back to its former owners before they could harvest their first crops.

Four million Black Americans were free from slavery, but they entered this new world almost entirely illiterate, owning nothing, and with no means to become economically independent. Many former slaves resorted to sharecropping, sometimes on the same plantations where they had been enslaved. They would farm the plantation owner's land in return for keeping a share of the crop at the end of the year.

Southern states passed a slew of laws known as "Black codes" to limit the rights of Black workers. They applied specifically to Black, but not White, people. One type was vagrancy laws. They required all Black men to sign an employment contract to work for a White employer at the beginning of each year. The contracts would prohibit workers from quitting or looking for other work with better pay. Any Black man not under a contract could be considered a vagrant and imprisoned. Another set of laws were apprenticeship laws. They allowed judges to force Black children to work, unpaid, for White employers under the pretext that the parents could not afford to support them.

The Black codes prohibited Black people from assembling in groups, from making public speeches without permission, and from owning firearms, swords, or even Bowie knives. They forbade Black people to travel without their White employer's permission, to testify against a White person, and to marry a White person. Many of the laws were written so broadly that virtually any dispute between a Black person and a White person could constitute breaking a law.

What happened when a Black person broke one of these laws? The Thirteenth Amendment outlawed slavery, but it contained a loophole. The text read: "Neither slavery nor involuntary servitude, except as a punishment for crime whereof the party shall have been duly convicted, shall exist within the United States, or any place subject to their jurisdiction." Those five words, "except as punishment for crime," were seized upon by southern states and became the basis for the convict leasing system. Once they were convicted of a crime, the "involuntary servitude" of Black prisoners could be leased by White employers, who paid the jailers a fee but paid the workers nothing. Although exact numbers are unknown, it is estimated that hundreds of thousands became victims of this system of "slavery by another name."

In 1866, Congress passed a Civil Rights Bill to strike back against the Black codes. It (along with the Fourteenth Amendment) said that anyone born in the United States was a citizen, regardless of race, color, or "previous condition of slavery or involuntary servitude." It asserted that any citizen could own property, make contracts, sue, and testify in court. Most important, it said that all laws apply equally to people regardless of race. Andrew Johnson vetoed the bill. Then Congress overrode his veto, the first time a president's veto was overridden in American history.

Congress moved on to the most explosive issue of all—the thing that had finally gotten Lincoln assassinated—the right to vote. After much struggle and debate over the wording of the Fifteenth Amendment, they decided in 1869 to keep it simple: "The right of citizens of the United States to vote shall not be denied or abridged by the United States or by any State on account of race, color, or previous condition of servitude."

The minimalist wording, focusing specifically on race and servitude, made the amendment easier to pass in Congress. But as several congressmen noted at the time, the wording also made it easy to circumvent. As predicted, southern states soon imposed literacy tests and poll taxes to make voting more burdensome. The price varied by state, but common tax charges were between $1 and $3. It may not sound like much, but when adjusted for inflation it would cost between $20 and $60 today. For newly freed people who owned virtually nothing, it was a staggering expense. The poll tax and literacy tests were also burdens for poor White people. Several states got around this problem by passing a "grandfather clause," which exempted people from paying the poll tax if they, or their ancestors, had been eligible to vote before Black people gained the vote. In other words, White people could avoid the poll tax.

Thus began the long history of passing laws that did not explicitly mention race but had the effect of disadvantaging Black people. These laws were incredibly effective at reducing voter registration among Black citizens. By 1910, only 15 percent of Black adults were registered to vote in Virginia and only 2 percent in Alabama and Mississippi.

From the distance of more than 150 years, it is easy to see how White southerners defended their psychological bottom line on these issues. Starting from the premise that they were good and reasonable people and their groups (other White southerners) were good and reasonable people, it was not hard to justify preserving the "southern way of life." One justification was that there was nothing illegal about requiring literacy or other educational standards to be met for voter registration. An educated electorate, they argued, would lead to wiser decisions. As for poll taxes, the Constitution explicitly grants the government the ability to tax citizens. And by the letter of the law, the laws were indeed race neutral on their face. Another common justification was that northern Republicans were only extending the franchise to Black voters for partisan advantage, because Black voters overwhelmingly preferred Republicans. Even if enforcing these laws required violence and vigilante justice, it was in service of a greater good, since only White people were competent, in White southerners' minds, to govern.

This justification process gave rise to many of the racial stereotypes that still permeate American culture. Southern employers tried to control and coerce Black laborers. When Black workers resisted, they were deemed lazy. Southern lawmakers created a byzantine web of laws that allowed Black people to be convicted for the flimsiest of reasons. Then they called Black people criminals. They took the status quo that they had created as the natural state of things. When Black people deviated from or resisted the status quo, it was interpreted as something wrong with the values of Black people, not the status quo.

The Reconstruction years were a turbulent and violent time, as southern Democrats settled into a long-term posture of resistance to the new power structures. In some areas, Black citizens, in coalition with White "scalawags," managed to vote effectively enough to elect sixteen Black U.S. congressmen and hundreds of state legislators. Yet at the same time, voter suppression laws were passed and vigilante groups, like the Red Shirts, the Knights of the White Camelia, and the notorious Ku Klux Klan, carried out campaigns of violence and intimidation. Following several egregious massacres of Black Americans, President Ulysses S. Grant sent federal troops to combat the Klan and related hate groups. And so a deadly game of cat and mouse ensued, in which hate groups used violence and the threat of violence to limit Black political power, and federal military power was used to keep the hate groups in check.

That all ended with the disputed presidential election of 1876. The Republican Rutherford B. Hayes competed against Democrat Samuel Tilden. In events that uncomfortably echo today's contested elections, the vote was too close to immediately call in South Carolina, Louisiana, and Florida. Both parties claimed victory and accused the other side of electoral fraud. The three states each sent two delegations of electors. Congress created a bipartisan commission in January 1877 to sort it out. They argued until March, when a compromise was reached. Hayes would be declared the winner. In return, Hayes would remove federal troops from southern states. With the troops withdrawn, the game of cat and mouse was over. Reconstruction had ended and the Jim Crow system took its place. The darkness of unchecked White supremacy closed in around Black southerners for a century.

HOW LINCOLN'S SLAVE MAP BECAME OUR POLITICAL MAP

The darkness did not descend uniformly. As with secession, the states that were more economically dependent on slavery developed harsher laws and informal rules. Even within the states, the counties and towns where slavery was more prevalent developed stricter levels of racial segregation and more brutal systems of enforcement. If you look at a map of lynchings in each county, it looks almost exactly like the map of enslaved populations in Figure 1.

Lynchings sometimes erupted spontaneously, but they were not random events. The most common accusation cited for lynchings was rape. But historical research indicates that rape allegations were used to describe nearly any close contact between Black men and White women. A man named William Brooks from Palestine, Arkansas, was lynched in 1894 after he asked his White employer for permission to marry the man's daughter. Thomas Miles was lynched in 1912 for inviting a White woman to have a cold drink. And a man named General Lee was lynched in Reevesville, South Carolina, in 1904 simply for knocking on the door of a White woman's house.

Besides the fear of social contact between Black and White people, the most common motives for lynching had to do with power. Some of the most frequent victims of lynching were political activists, labor organizers, or people who did not show sufficient deference to White people. People like Jesse Thornton, who was lynched in Luverne, Alabama, in 1940 for referring to a White police officer by his name rather than "mister." Lynching was, foremost, a means of enforcing the racial hierarchy. That was most important in areas that had previously depended the most on slavery. Around four thousand racially motivated lynchings are believed to have occurred between 1877 and 1940. The more people were enslaved in a county in 1860, the more people were lynched there following Reconstruction. An increase of 10 percent in the previously enslaved population of an area is associated with about two additional lynchings per one hundred thousand people.

The racial hierarchy that lynchings protected is still with us, and the fingerprint of slavery can still be seen clearly in its patterns. For example, throughout the Jim Crow era, southern towns designated which parts of town were "Black" neighborhoods and which were "White" neighborhoods. When schools were built to educate Black children, the schools were segregated into Black schools and White schools. The segregation of the Jim Crow era is obvious. But what is less obvious is that those same places are more segregated today.

Segregation in housing and schools changes very slowly, because once an area was designated as the Black part of town, it was also the poor area of town. Once some areas are known as Black neighborhoods, few White homebuyers want to move in there. And once some areas are known as White neighborhoods, the higher property values keep lower-income people out, who are disproportionately Black. Even if not for the many blatant and subtle ways that Black homebuyers are excluded from White neighborhoods, the economic disparity alone would keep them segregated for decades.

Generations later, the property values in the White and Black parts of town remain very different. And the Black-majority schools, which are near the Black-majority neighborhoods, still have less funding than White-majority schools today, because schools are funded in large part by local property taxes. This arrangement guarantees that discrimination against one generation will turn into unequal opportunities for future generations.

And it does. Research from my lab and others suggests that counties that had more slavery in 1860 not only have more segregation; they also have more Black residents in poverty today. Black residents in those counties today also have lower economic mobility, meaning that children born into poverty are less likely to escape poverty as adults. Meanwhile, White residents in counties that relied more on slavery have higher average incomes today.

How can the racial inequality that was put in place more than 150 years ago still be with us? Americans like to believe that individual hard work and talent are the main drivers of success. But even the most individualistic observer will admit that in reality, economic success or failure is driven by at least three factors: starting advantages, individual hard work and talent, and random chance. The relative importance of these three factors has been a matter of much debate among opinion writers. But for empirically minded scientists, it's not controversial.

Scores of studies have found that about half of a person's economic outcomes are due to their parents' income, wealth, and education. One remarkable study managed to use tax data from Florence, Italy, in 1427 (twenty-five years before Leonardo da Vinci was born!) and match the names to their descendants in 2011. After nearly six hundred years, the descendants of the wealthiest Florentines still owned 12 percent more wealth than the descendants of poor Florentines. Similar long-term-wealth persistence has been found in England and Sweden.

This kind of persistence cannot be explained by genetic heritability of traits, like intelligence, because each generation shares 50 percent of its genes with their parents. The whole biological point of sexual reproduction is to reshuffle the genome in each generation. You share 50 percent of your DNA with your parents, 25 percent with your grandparents, and so on. After seven generations, we share less than 1 percent of our DNA with any given ancestor. And yet, after more than twenty generations, our ancestors' wealth is still shaping the economic advantages and disadvantages we are born with. Wealth is more heritable than DNA.

Income and wealth inheritances can be more powerful than individual talent. Children from affluent families who have below-average achievement test scores still have a seven in ten chance of reaching the top quartile of income and education. Children from low-income families with above-average test scores, on the other hand, have only a three in ten chance of reaching the top quartile. In other words, it is better to be born rich than smart.

It's not that talent doesn't matter—children with above-average test scores are about twice as likely as those with below-average scores to end up in the top income quartile. But the influence of talent is swamped by the massive impact of starting advantages and disadvantages. For kids whose parents are in the top fifth of the income distribution, about 80 percent will go to a four-year college. But for kids who grow up in the bottom fifth, only about 36 percent will attend college. We can predict an unborn child's outcomes, like college graduation and adult income, with great accuracy simply by knowing the zip code they are about to be born into.

When I explain this research in talks, people often point out counterexamples. Sometimes it's someone they know who was born poor but worked their way up. Sometimes it's themselves or their parents. Sometimes it's me. This kind of counterexample amounts to cherry-picking anecdotes that don't reflect the broader reality. It's like arguing against the generalization that men tend to be taller than women by pointing to one tall woman. People in general—and Americans in particular—like to believe that we make our own success through hard work. But the data is clear that starting advantages and disadvantages are even more powerful. Because of this, one generation's inequality of outcomes becomes the next generation's inequality of opportunity.

Most Black families in the United States started over with nothing just two or three lifetimes ago. Regardless of laws banning racial discrimination that took effect fewer than sixty years ago, the cumulative effects of those disadvantages are profound. Even if discrimination magically stopped the moment the Civil Rights Act passed, those vast advantages and disadvantages would persist. Discrimination didn't magically disappear, of course. In a project led by Manuel Galvan, we analyzed every field experiment on racial discrimination in hiring and housing since the year 2000. These field experiments sent job applications or rental applications to real employers or landlords, and randomly assigned the race of the applicant to appear either Black or White. Across more than two hundred studies, we found that Black applicants were discriminated against between 10 and 20 percent of the time. It was not just a few "bad apples" discriminating. Instead, statistical simulations suggested that the typical decision-maker tended to discriminate a bit for each decision, putting a constant thumb on the scale in favor of White applicants over Black applicants. The cumulative effects of being discriminated against a little bit, again and again, at each choice point, are devastating.

The median income for Black families is about 60 percent lower than that for White families. But the gap is much more dramatic for wealth. The net worth of the average White family is about ten times that of the average Black family. About 30 percent of White families receive an inheritance, but only about 10 percent of Black families do. Among those who do inherit, the amount for White families is twice as much. And even when wealth is not transmitted directly through inheritance, wealthy families spend five times as much as poor families on education and enrichment activities for their children. All these dynamics explain why we can so clearly see the patterning of racial inequality today based on the dependence on slavery in 1860.

I am not talking about some vague difference between the

North and the South. As you can see in the map in Figure 1, some areas like northern Alabama, western North Carolina, and eastern Tennessee had fewer slaves than other areas that were equally far south. We found striking differences in segregation and racial disparities based on the practice of slavery from one county to the next, even within the same states.

Consider the difference between Wilmington and Asheville, both midsize cities in North Carolina. Wilmington is near the coast, where flat land allowed cotton plantations to thrive. It became the largest and richest city in the state in the late 1800s. For two decades following the Civil War, Black and White merchants became prosperous, and some Black politicians became powerful—until a White supremacist coup d'état toppled the government in 1890 and succeeded in restoring White domination that lasted until the civil rights movement seventy years later.

Asheville is in the west, in the southern part of the Appalachian Mountains called the Blue Ridge. The altitude meant the area was not submerged during much of the Cretaceous period, and the terrain became unsuitable for cotton. Because of that, slavery was not widespread in the area. Walking around these two cities, both affluent vacation destinations today, you can feel the difference. Wilmington is visibly more segregated by race and income than Asheville. Wilmington has a beautiful cobblestone downtown. But the upscale restaurants, bars, and cafés feel completely separated from the parts of town where the pawn shops and check-cashing places dominate. In Asheville, the poor parts of town mix low-income housing with artists' studios and food trucks. It is a big boiling cauldron of humanity of all colors and styles, wandering up and down the steep slanted streets where bars and bookstores and barbershops keep their lights on late.

When people see this kind of racial segregation and inequality, what do they think it means? Do they interpret it as advantages and disadvantages passed down through the generations? Or do they see it as an example of Black people lacking ability or just not working hard enough to succeed? Our research suggests that the answer depends on the race of the person doing the interpreting. We used the population data from the 1860 census captured in Lincoln's map, along with data on housing segregation, race differences in poverty, and upward mobility, to predict the racial attitudes of people in each county today.

We measured racial attitudes in two ways. The first was a simple rating scale in which research participants rate how warm or cold their feelings are toward White and Black people in general. That measure is simple and easy to understand, but it is also easy to answer in a way that presents you in a positive light. Many people are careful on that kind of measure to avoid being seen as prejudiced. The second measure was a computerized test that is harder to manipulate to make yourself look good. It was an implicit bias test that measures how quickly respondents can sort the labels "Black people" and "White people" together with good and bad words. The more closely a person associates the racial groups with good and bad evaluations in their cognitive network, the faster they can sort them together.

Both measures of racial attitudes showed the same pattern. In counties that had more slavery in 1860, current-day White residents had more negative attitudes toward Black people. Again, it was not a general North/South difference. Counties and towns within the same states, like Wilmington and Asheville, differed substantially in their attitudes based on the prevalence of slavery.

But how can history from a century and a half ago influence

the attitudes of people today? We found that the link was modern-day segregation and racial inequality. Places that were more dependent on slavery in 1860 developed more segregation, and that segregation is still palpable today, with mostly Black neighborhoods and White neighborhoods. Counties that depended more on slavery set in motion disadvantages for Black Americans that can still be detected in higher poverty rates and lower upward mobility for Black Americans today. And it was these modern-day racial inequalities that cued anti-Black attitudes in the minds of White residents (but not Black residents) today.

Black residents tend to look at that inequality and see evidence of discrimination, in line with the mounds of evidence just reviewed. That interpretation suits their psychological bottom line, but it is also consistent with the history and the evidence. But when the average White American looks around and sees the inequalities and disadvantages that were set in motion by hundreds of years of slavery and discrimination, they feel a greater conflict. To make sense of that inequality while preserving their view that they and their groups are good and reasonable, they need to engage in some cognitive contortions. The most common contortion is to conclude that the inequality is a result of something wrong with Black people.

Psychologist Nicolas Sommet and I compiled the results of several large national surveys of how Americans explain racial gaps in income and wealth. In counties where the poverty rate was higher among Black residents, Black residents were more likely to explain Black poverty as a result of discrimination and lack of opportunity. White residents, on the other hand, showed the opposite pattern. The greater the Black poverty rates, the more they chalked up racial gaps to internal traits like laziness or unintelligence. Ironically, the more discrimination there is, the more White residents are likely to see Black failings.

Another study gets even more directly at how people make political meaning of the racial inequality around them. Political scientists Avidit Acharya, Matthew Blackwell, and Maya Sen looked at how patterns of slavery predict today's racial and political beliefs. They correlated the enslaved populations in each county from the 1860 census with responses on a measure of racial attitudes that is often called "racial resentment." But that's a bit of a misnomer, because it doesn't actually ask about resenting people based on race.

The scale asks whether you agree or disagree with statements like: "Generations of slavery and discrimination have created conditions that make it difficult for blacks to work their way out of the lower class." Another statement reads: "It's really a matter of some people just not trying hard enough: if blacks would only try harder they could be just as well off as whites." That is to say, the scale measures whether people believe that racial inequalities are mainly due to slavery and discrimination or to Black people not working hard enough. For people who believe that inequality is due to past and present discrimination, the world around them is an uneven playing field. To achieve fairness, active steps need to be taken to provide extra resources and opportunities to Black citizens. But for those who deny the importance of discrimination, the field is level already. Any attempts to level it further are seen as illegitimate "handouts" or even "reverse discrimination."

Acharya and his colleagues found that in counties with more slavery in 1860, White respondents more strongly endorsed the idea that a lack of hard work, rather than discrimination, explained racial inequality. Once again, the places where slavery and discrimination were the most intensive are the places where modern-day White residents deny the importance of slavery and discrimination the most. They look around at the massive levels of racial inequality and make sense of it in ways that protect their psychological bottom line.

The stakes are high, because the belief that inequality is the fault of Black people rather than past and present discrimination turns out to be the single strongest factor separating Republicans and Democratic voters today. Among people who "strongly agreed" that inequality was due to Black people not working hard enough, more than 90 percent voted for Donald Trump in 2020. And among those who "strongly agreed" that discrimination was the reason for inequality, more than 90 percent voted for Joe Biden. (See Figure 2 on the next page.)

Racial attitudes are not the only group-based attitude that matters for politics, but they are the most potent. People who have negative attitudes toward one out-group tend to have negative attitudes toward other ones too. A classic study from the 1940s first demonstrated this. The researchers asked White American participants to rate their feelings toward lots of different groups, including Black Americans, Jews, Polish people, Armenians, and so on. They found that participants who disliked one out-group tended to dislike the other out-groups as well.

In a sneaky twist, the researchers embedded a few groups in the list that don't exist, like "Pireneans." Although the participants had presumably never heard of those groups, they rated them anyway. And those who disliked Black people, Jews, and Poles also disliked Pireneans. Researchers today find that people who have negative attitudes toward Black Americans also tend to dislike Hispanics, immigrants, Muslims, and other out-groups. And yet, because

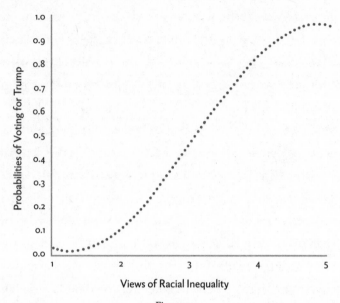

Figure 2.
Probability of voting for Donald Trump plotted against views on racial inequality.
Data from the American National Election Studies. Graph created by the author.

of America's unique history with slavery and the inequality that followed, attitudes toward Black Americans remain the strongest predictor of how Americans vote.

Acharya and his colleagues' research confirmed this relationship: the more slavery was practiced in 1860, the more today's White residents vote for Republican candidates and the more Black respondents vote for Democrats. This is not new with Donald Trump. Racial attitudes were a strong predictor of voting at least since the 2000 election and have gradually become stronger in each election since then. It is a trend that has been strengthening for decades, as our partisan identities have come to orbit our racial identities more and more.

No other variable comes close to explaining the partisan gap as strongly as views on the legitimacy of racial inequality. It was a

stronger predictor than beliefs about taxes or government regulation, free trade, same-sex marriage, abortion, or any of the typical
issues-based measures that are often used to explain why people
vote. The favorite explanation among pundits for why nearly half
of Americans support Donald Trump is "economic anxiety." It
seems plausible that working-class Americans left behind by glob-
alization, technological changes, and skyrocketing economic inequality might turn to a disruptive leader. They might like the way
that he breaks norms, acts crudely, and generally gives a middle
finger to the elites who talk politely but don't change anything.
Multiple studies now have made head-to-head comparisons between the economic anxiety explanation and the racial inequality
explanation. In every one, it is views of racial inequality that turn
out to be the strong predictor of Trump support and of Republican
Party identification more generally.

For ordinary voters, today's political parties are, in large part, a
proxy for whether people believe the racial status quo is legitimate.
If you were born into a family that identifies as Black, the likelihood that you support Democrats is about 90 percent. If you were
born into a family that identifies as White, the likelihood that you
support Republicans is about 60 percent. And if you were born
into a White family in a place that was covered in microscopic seashells a hundred million years ago, that probability is much higher.
Acharya's work suggests that the proportion is around 80 percent in
counties that previously had the largest enslaved populations.

When Edmund Burke was writing in the late 1700s, upholding
the traditional social order meant supporting the monarchy and
the Church as the legitimate sources of power. Today's conservatives also want to uphold the traditional power structures, but it is
not a monarchy they support (we will examine religion in chapter 7).

Today the hierarchy that most strongly separates Republicans and Democrats is the racial hierarchy. Recall that in chapter 3 we saw that most aspects of ideologies are logically inconsistent and unstable for most people, but racial attitudes were an exception. Views of racial inequality provide the closest thing that most people have to an ideology, and it organizes the way they think about other issues that would uphold or diminish racial hierarchies.

In a study of welfare attitudes, for example, Jazmin Brown-Iannuzzi and I measured how strongly participants supported increasing or decreasing welfare benefits such as food and cash assistance to poor families. Then we asked participants to consider whom they expected would benefit from the policy. We used a task in which participants selected a series of photos that matched their mental images of welfare recipients. Each individual photo was just slightly different from the other photos, so participants were not aware of what patterns they might be revealing in their choices. After the study was over, we morphed the images together to reconstruct their mental images. For respondents who wanted to reduce welfare spending, their mental images clearly depicted Black men—even though the most common recipients of welfare benefits in the United States are White women.

We conducted another study using the same methods to examine the mental images underpinning support for voter identification laws. Advocates of these laws argue that they stop fraudulent voting without unfairly reducing the voting power of particular groups such as Black or lower-income voters. Critics of the laws argue that they function like poll taxes—they are race-neutral on their face but have the effect of reducing voting among poor and Black people, who are less likely to have valid IDs. When we asked participants to decide which people looked like illegitimate voters, the images they generated were clear. The more they supported voter ID laws, the more their mental images of illegitimate voters depicted Black people.

WHO, ME, RACIST?

Democrats calling Republicans racist has become a cliché. Republicans generally understand the accusation in a narrow way, as saying that they personally have hateful attitudes toward Black individuals. In this view, someone who is racist would be consistently mean to any Black person they meet. The average Republican voter doesn't recognize those hateful feelings in themselves at all. This is why saying "Some of my best friends are Black" or "I voted for a Black Republican candidate" seems like a reasonable defense to some but makes liberals roll their eyes. What counts as "racism" is itself part of a person's beliefs about whether racial inequality is legitimate.

Social scientists distinguish between individual racism and systemic racism. Individual racism is about a person's attitudes and feelings toward other people based on race. Systemic racism, on the other hand, is simply the sum of a few empirical facts. First, historical and present discrimination left Black people, on average, with lower wealth, poorer schools, less political power, and fewer opportunities than White people on average. Second, those inequalities cause differential opportunities for future generations. And third, some kinds of laws and policies have the effect of maintaining those inequalities while other laws and policies diminish them.

Wealth disparities between Black and White families were created through laws and policies. Neighborhoods and schools were racially segregated by laws and policies, and they are still segregated. Voting power among Black Americans was reduced, first through explicitly discriminatory laws and then through laws that were race-neutral on their face but discriminatory in their effect. Poll taxes and grandfather clauses are no longer legal, but voting access laws and gerrymandered voter districts have the same kinds of unequal impacts today.

The major source of division between Republicans and Democrats is whether they find these unequal arrangements to be legitimate. That is why the racial resentment measure is such a powerful predictor of partisanship. It measures an individual's attitudes, but it asks about whether they find systemic racism acceptable. Those who score low think existing racial disparities are illegitimate, and that it is everyone's responsibility to do something about it. Those who score high on racial resentment deny that discrimination is to blame and think Black people should simply work harder.

Academics have argued for decades about whether that kind of measure should be called "racism" or not. I would say it is a form of racism to deny the overwhelming evidence of discrimination and its consequences and instead blame Black individuals for inequality. But some scholars, especially those on the right, think that calling the attitudes measured by the racial resentment scale racism stigmatizes the conservative worldview, which respects traditional hierarchies and emphasizes individual effort. This back-and-forth reminds me of a time in a graduate school seminar when we were discussing the difference between individual prejudice and systemic racism. One student, a White man, seemed distressed about the idea of systemic racism. Finally, he blurted out, "But . . . if we define racism that way, then conservatives are, by definition, racist!" Across the room, a Black woman answered with a slow, resonating, "Mmmmm-hmmmm."

Most accounts of the role of racial resentment in political attitudes stop at the strong correlation between the two. But that hesitation just raises the question of why some people score high on racial resentment and others score low. Even the most bigoted person is not a cartoon villain, being mean just for the sake of being mean. They are trying to make sense of the world and their place in it while maintaining that they are a good and reasonable person and their groups are too. Racism isn't a very satisfactory explanation for human behavior. Racism is often what needs to be explained if we want to make sense of people's actions.

Understanding the historical and psychological reasons why some people come to view racial inequality as illegitimate whereas others come to view it as a legitimate outcome of a meritocracy offers much more insight. Regardless of which side you are on, you probably feel you are dispassionately weighing the evidence. And yet, we can predict which evidence you will find persuasive if we know only the racial group you were born into and the amount of chalk in the soil where you were born. To understand how both of these things can be true at the same time, it helps to remember Lincoln's words: "They are just what we would be in their situation." We are following paths laid down for us millions of years ago, all the while feeling that we are simply seeing reality as it is. Our psychological immune systems won't have it any other way.

FIVE

GODDAMNED DOCTORS
AND LAWYERS

*The paradox of education is precisely this—that
as one begins to become conscious one begins to
examine the society in which he is being educated.*

—JAMES BALDWIN

I 've lost my southern accent, and lately I've been wanting it back. But it's not that easy. There were times in grad school when I would intentionally suppress my accent, copying other students who sounded like newscasters. I thought it would make me sound more intelligent. A professor in graduate school once said to me, "You don't sound Kentuckian, you sound pretty articulate to me." Another asked if I slipped into southern dialect when I was tired because a southern dialect is "cognitively simpler." I got the message that certain accents didn't belong in academia. But in retrospect, what I was really pretending to be was middle class. I accustomed myself to a new accent the way I learned to like wine. Gradually, I stopped the imitation and effortlessly talked like someone from anywhere.

But we don't directly choose our accents, any more than we

choose our social class. By the time I sounded like I was middle class, I actually was. I had a doctorate and an assistant professor job, and I genuinely liked wine. By then, everyone I knew talked like me—or rather, I talked like them.

Accents tend to drift toward a person's peer group. That's why children sometimes have accents very different from their parents. You can tell who people are trying to fit in with by their accents. When my siblings get together, you can tell by their accents who went away to college and how far they moved. But the accents were there, at least in part, before we ever left for college. Without knowing it, we were tuning ourselves, even as children, for different social-class groups, and therefore different political identities.

If race is the most powerful social identity dividing our politics, then social class is not far behind. But the role of class in political divisions is muddy and confused in most popular writing. News stories are filled with descriptions of "working-class" Trump voters and "coastal elites" who make up the Democratic Party. We see stories about "economic anxiety" leading former Democratic voters to switch to Republicans. The bestselling book *What's the Matter with Kansas?* tackled the puzzle of why poor Americans in flyover country vote Republican, against their economic self-interests. The answer suggested in the book was that Republican leaders distracted those voters by riling them up with messages about religion, guns, and gay rights. Social issues, in other words, blinded them to their own economic interests.

This view that poor people vote Republican is a popular one, but it is simply not supported by the data. In fact, it gets the relationship between social class and political identities almost entirely backward. To understand why, we need to unpack what social class means.

The most influential scholar for the modern concept of social class was the German sociologist Max Weber. He argued that social inequalities can be broken down into three sources. The first is how a person fares in the economic marketplace. He called this "klassen," which is translated as "class," but what he had in mind was money. The second piece was social status, which reflected how much honor, respect, or scorn a person receives from their community. And the third piece was whether someone belongs to a political party that held a lot of power. In other words, if you want to know where someone stands in society, you need to ask about their wealth, their social status, and their political power.

Weber was a sophisticated theorist, and his writings have been scrutinized by generations of scholars to understand the subtle shades of meaning in his prose. But as sociology evolved from a mostly philosophical field to an empirical social science, the fine-grained distinctions of scholars like Weber did not always translate very well to survey research. By the 1930s and '40s, Weber's verbal categories started morphing into a new hybrid term: *socioeconomic status*. This unwieldy word is an attempt to capture the first two of Weber's categories—social status together with economic means. By the 1960s, socioeconomic status (or SES for short) became the dominant term for social scientists studying social class. And as survey research and polling developed into mature scientific methods, socioeconomic status came to be measured mainly by two questions: *What is your income?* and *What is your level of education?*

Squeezing these two questions together and combining them into a single measure is a way of recognizing that income and education tend to go together. They are in fact tightly correlated. In 2020, the median yearly income for high school graduates was about $39,000. But for college graduates it was $65,000, and for those with doctoral-level degrees, it was $98,000. And yet, despite this strong link on average, they do not always go together. Plenty of college grads go to work in a service or retail job that doesn't pay much. And lots of high school dropouts have gone on to earn millions by starting their own businesses.

Merging income and education together creates even more confusion when it comes to politics, because income and education actually work in opposite directions politically. According to exit polls in the 2020 election, voters with incomes below $50,000 voted for Joe Biden by a 55 to 44 percent margin. Those with incomes above $100,000 voted for Donald Trump by a similar margin, 54 to 42 percent. This trend is not new with Trump, but has been in place for decades. The image of the poor American voting Republican against their economic interests gets it exactly backward. The poor favor Democrats and the wealthy favor Republicans.

Education, on the other hand, favors Democrats. Among voters with a high school diploma or less, only 41 percent voted for Joe Biden. But Biden was the choice among 56 percent of those with a bachelor's degree, and 67 percent of those with an advanced degree. The education gap is huge—it's about as large as the margin by which White voters prefer Republicans or Hispanic voters prefer Democrats. When news stories report on "working-class" people voting Republican, they are talking about "non-college" voters, to use the phrase popular among pollsters. Separating income from education is important for understanding what is really going on here.

WHAT'S THE MATTER WITH MANHATTAN?

The income effect is the more straightforward part. Republican leaders tend to cut taxes, especially for the wealthy, and cut benefits to the poor. Democrats tend to do the reverse. Both sides tell stories about how their policies really help everyone, of course. But to the extent that people vote on their beliefs about those policies, they seem to believe that Republicans are better for the interests of higher earners and Democrats are better for the interests of low earners.

Most of the data on the income-partisanship relationship is correlational. So it is hard to know whether income shapes partisanship, whether partisanship shapes people's earnings, or whether some other factor shapes both. There are a few studies, however, that help identify what causes what. In chapter 3 I described my lab's research finding that randomly assigning participants to "win" at an economic game shifted their political attitudes toward a more conservative view about taxes and benefits. That research suggests that when people become wealthier, they might become more conservative.

A fascinating series of studies of lottery winners confirms that intuition. These studies, one in the United States and one in the UK, tracked lottery winners to see if they became more conservative after they won, in comparison to nonwinners. Lotteries are excellent natural experiments because the outcomes are truly random. The winners are not different from the losers in any respect other than the luck of the win, so the differences between groups cannot be explained by education, hard work, or other differences between individuals. Sure enough, lottery winners started voting for more conservative candidates and parties, and the larger their win, the more conservative they became.

The lottery winners are unlikely to say they shifted to voting conservative because they wanted to pay less tax. Instead, they are likely to argue that low taxes are better for the entire economy, they create jobs, and that a rising tide lifts all boats. Once again, people's behavior is easier to understand if we separate their reasons from the causes of their reasons. In these studies, economic self-interest caused people to discover new reasons to support conservative tax policies.

Some poor people do vote Republican, just as some rich people vote Democrat. But these individuals are the exception rather than the rule. In this light, there is nothing the matter with Kansas in terms of voting against self-interest. It is just as fitting to ask "What's the matter with Manhattan?" where many wealthy professionals vote for Democrats, who might raise their taxes. Still, in many cases the cause is not the money, but rather the differences in education that tend to go with higher or lower incomes. The diploma divide is even larger than the income divide, but it is also more complex and interesting. Let's start with water witching.

THE DIPLOMA DIVIDE

Witching for water will change the way you look at your hands. There are different ways you can do it. Two wire clothes hangers bent into L-shaped rods will work. Or you can buy precisely machined copper rods on the internet. But Dad always used a tree branch. He'd find a Y-shaped branch on a sapling with smooth bark and cut it down with his pocket knife. You hold on to the two forks of the Y with your palms turned up, and let the long part point in front of you. Then you walk slowly across the grass in a grid pattern. That's the way I learned it.

First I watched him walk, one step at a time, in a long straight line across the yard. His hands were holding both ends of the branch, leaving his cigarette dangling from his lips. The rod started to dip, and he tightened his grip to hold it in place. Each step after that, the tip of the rod pulled down until it was pointing straight toward the ground. "That's where she is," he said out of the corner of his mouth. Then he opened his hands to show the bark, now twisted off in his palms.

"Give her a try," he said, handing me the rod. "Let's see if you've got it." I wrapped my hands tight around the ends of the branch and retraced his steps, two of my small strides for every one of his. As I approached the spot where the rod had dipped for him, I felt nothing. I prepared myself for the disappointment. I probably didn't have it. And then, the rod started to quiver. I tightened my grip, not wanting him to think I was faking. But the tighter I squeezed, the more the rod twisted inside my clenched fists. Each step forward, the tip of the rod pulled farther down, until at last I stopped, the rod pointing straight down to the same spot where Dad had stopped. "Well I'll be damned," he laughed, "looks like you've got it too." I opened my hands, some of the bark still in my palms.

"How does it work?" I demanded.

"Electricity," he said. He explained that all living things transmitted electric currents. Muscles, brains, they all work through electricity. And for some people—the ones who have the gift like us—the electricity in their bodies resonates with the electricity in the tree branch and the current of flowing water under the ground. "It's like magnets," he said.

"Like magnets," I repeated, still staring at my hands. We drove a stake in the ground to mark the spot, and the next day Dad and my older brother drilled the well. By suppertime they were pumping clean water.

Water witching (also called dowsing or divining) is an ancient practice. In Europe, there are references dating back to the fifteenth century, when German miners used forked branches to choose where to dig. Martin Luther criticized it because he thought it was the devil's magic.

Water and minerals are not the only hidden finds turned up this way. In 1692, a peasant named Jacques Aymar in Lyon, France, developed a reputation for solving murders using a divining rod. When thieves broke into a local wine shop and stole five hundred livres, they bludgeoned the owner and his wife to death, leaving no witnesses. The police called on Aymar for help when their investigation hit a dead end. His rod led them on an excursion down the Rhône to a small town called Beaucaire, where nineteen-year-old Joseph Arnoul sat in a jail cell for petty theft. Arnoul denied the charges, but the rod kept pointing at him. After a brief trial, the teenager was convicted of murder and executed by being broken on the wheel.

Today it is rare for police to enlist the help of witchers, but witching for water remains widespread. Sometimes people even use divining rods for oil and gas exploration. A couple of years after we drilled that water well, Dad and a friend decided to develop their talent for water witching into something more profitable—witching for oil. "Geologists don't know what they're doing anyway," he said. "Half of their wells turn up dry. They're no better than the goddamned doctors and lawyers charging three hundred dollars an hour to tell you what you already know."

They reasoned that a tree branch worked for finding water because wood is itself full of water. So to find oil they needed to make a rod that contained oil. They bought a pile of plastic tubing and pipes and fasteners from the hardware store, then spent their weekends for more than a year tinkering with ways to build a plastic forked rod that had the flexibility and feel of a sapling branch. It was made of hollow tubing, which was filled with crude oil.

To test whether it worked, they would drive to the site of an active oil well. Kentucky is not a major oil-producing state, but there are productive wells scattered throughout the countryside. I begged Dad to let me come along, and once he did. We drove twenty minutes into the country and turned down a dirt road between two tobacco fields. An area of one of the fields had been cleared, and there sat a pump jack churning quietly away. It was a tall rig, with what looked like a giant hammer nodding slowly up and down, turned by a piston from a rotating engine below. At the top was a vertical pipe with a flame blazing like a torch, burning off the methane produced when the oil was pumped up.

To test the rod, Dad would walk toward the pump jack from different positions. As he got closer, the rod would begin to dip. By the time he was standing in front of the well, it was pointing toward the ground just as with the water in our backyard. If their artificial divining rod could detect the oil beneath this rig, they figured, it could find oil that had not yet been discovered.

So they set about witching for oil, putting on demonstrations of their rod's accuracy for investors and raising money to drill the well and buy the mineral rights to the most promising places. The investors were friends of friends, not professional oil men. Most of them were skeptical, but some found the electricity theory and the demonstrations convincing. By the end of that summer, they had drilled one oil well as a proof of concept. But the well was dry. They used every last dollar they had raised to drill a little deeper, and then a little deeper still, because the rod still pointed at that spot.

Many years later, in graduate school, I would learn about the larger history of witching, beyond the stories that had been handed down to me. I would learn about the principle of ideomotor action, which means that thinking about a movement or focusing our attention on a particular spot leads people to make subtle unconscious movements in that direction. And I would learn about the way that people generate the feeling of conscious control over their actions by observing the tight connection between thinking about an action and actually performing it.

The pointing end of a witching rod is longer than the handle ends, which means that a tiny movement of the hand can translate into a big swing at the tip. And the curve of the branch means that twists of the hands inward toward each other or outward away from each other create up-and-down swings at the tip. That instability creates an awkward feeling of disconnection between movements of the hands and the movement of the long end of the rod.

Psychologist Daniel Wegner showed how that disconnection makes people feel less control over the rod than with ordinary movements. We judge the causation of our own thoughts and actions the same way we judge the causation of one billiard ball hitting another. We can't see causation itself. We have to infer it. We see one ball roll into another, just before the second ball rolls across the table. Normally, our attention and thoughts and actions all go together like one ball hitting another. We look at a coffee cup that we want to pick up and think about picking it up, and our hand moves to pick it up.

A witching rod scrambles that pairing between thought and action. When you focus on a particular spot, you subtly move the rod toward it, while at the same time thinking that you are actually resisting its pull. When you squeeze the rod, it doesn't stop. When you bend it inward, the tip moves up or down. It's the same principle as trying to hold a pendulum perfectly still, or using a Ouija board with a partner. We contribute unintentionally to the movement while feeling we are not causing the movement.

I would later learn that scads of studies had been conducted testing the accuracy of witching, dowsing, and divining techniques, and the results showed that accuracy is no better than blind guesses under carefully controlled laboratory conditions. Only when the witcher already knew where their target was hidden did they "discover" it more accurately than chance. So why the high accuracy when finding water but not oil? It was because in most parts of the United States, water is nearly everywhere underground, but oil is not. We could have chosen anywhere to sink that well in our backyard and we would have found water.

What we needed was a "control group"—a place where there was no water underground. We needed random assignment of witching attempts to the water-present and water-absent conditions. We needed double-blind testing, in which neither the witcher nor the experimenter knew which condition had water, to avoid subtle unintentional biases. And we needed to repeat the trial hundreds or thousands of times to separate lucky guesses from real accuracy. In other words, we needed the techniques that separate scientific inquiry from intuitive tinkering.

Dad and I were fooled by our experience, but I don't think we were being stupid or foolish. Before I knew about ideomotor effects and the way that perceptions of action control work, the resonating electricity theory was the best way I had to make sense of my experience. After I learned about the scientific findings, they became the best explanations. The science could explain both why the rod doesn't work under conditions that don't allow you to fool yourself, and also why it felt so vividly real. One thing that higher education does is to make our experiences something to be explained, as opposed to making experiences the explanations.

Now I use witching rods as demonstrations in my psychology classes. I throw my keys on the ground, and demonstrate how to find them with the rod. Then it's the students' turn. Students routinely feel the irresistible pull of the rod, sometimes to the point that bark twists off in their hands. But only, of course, if they can see where the keys are laying. We use the demonstration as a conversation starter for talking about science and intuition and the ways that we can fool ourselves.

Imagine if some know-it-all professor had tried to explain to us at the time that water witching had been debunked in scientific tests. Maybe they explained to us about control groups and double-blind trials and unintentional biases. There is little chance my Dad or I would have been persuaded. For one thing, understanding scientific methods takes months or years for students to master through study and practice. And even more important, we had experienced the astonishing twisting of the rod for ourselves. It felt amazing, and it revealed that I had a special gift that Dad and I shared. Abstractions like those scientific findings would pale in comparison to the vividness and power of our firsthand experiences. After all, we knew we were good and reasonable people. The idea that we were fooling ourselves would have been incompatible with that deep knowledge. We would have dismissed the professor along with the goddamned doctors, lawyers, and geologists.

Higher education creates a chasm that is hard to cross. The highly educated spend years studying history, science, math, literature, and so on. They practice understanding that the way we do things in our particular time and place is nothing special—it's just one moment in history and one culture among thousands. That attitude can be offensive to people who have learned to invest their identity in their particular time and place and culture.

University education teaches people to question their assumptions. Students practice setting aside their intuitive experience to think using formal rules and procedures. In my first year of college, I kept encountering puzzles posed by professors or textbooks that pitted intuitions against logic or data. A problem I encountered in an early psychology class, for example, was Daniel Kahneman and Amos Tversky's famous Linda Problem. It goes like this:

Linda is thirty-one years old, single, outspoken, and very bright. She majored in philosophy. As a student, she was deeply concerned with issues of discrimination and social justice, and also participated in anti-nuclear demonstrations. Which is more likely: that Linda is a bank teller or that Linda is a bank teller and is active in the feminist movement?

Intuition pulls for the second answer because her background description seems similar to someone who would be a feminist. And yet, the correct answer is that she is more likely to be a bank teller, because the set of people who are feminist bank tellers is a subset of the people who are bank tellers. So any given person is more likely to be from the larger set than the smaller subset.

Learning to approach everyday questions as logic or math problems is very different from the way ordinary people without a university education think. As a kid, I had been taught to do the opposite, prioritizing intuitions, stories, authority figures, or "common sense." In my Catholic grade school, for example, I was taught that God the Father, Jesus, and the Holy Spirit were each separate persons, and each was fully God, and yet together they were all one God. They were not one third of a God each, and yet together they made one God. The Trinity poses a logical contradiction, because one plus one plus one equals three, not one. And yet, we were taught that Church authority is to be trusted over our mere mortal reason. To trust reason over divine revelation was arrogant and sinful.

Problems like the Trinity suggest an easy intuitive answer (it's three in one) followed by a slow, logical rethinking (wait, that adds up to three, not one) and finally shift away from reason back to a larger sense of intuition (it's beyond human reason—just trust the mystery!). Problems like the Linda Problem, on the other hand, suggest an easy intuitive solution, followed by a careful, logical rethinking, and that's it. When I first encountered those kinds of problems, I kept expecting there to be a final third act, in which deeply felt intuitions were vindicated after all. But there never was. The lesson I learned in college was that when intuitions conflict with reason or evidence, intuition is mistaken. In fact, you can use reason and evidence to understand why your intuition felt right but was actually wrong.

After years of practicing this unnatural way of thinking, highly educated people often forget how they used to think, relying heavily on stories and intuitions and vivid experiences. It's like spending years learning to speak French and then yelling at someone who doesn't speak French to just speak French, dammit.

One summer while I was home from college, Dad was considering trading in his old car for a Dodge with lower mileage. When he started his sales job in the 1960s, the company provided him with a car. He spent his days driving from one rural diner, school, or hospital kitchen to another, selling frozen food. In the nineties, they stopped providing the company car and instead paid him a weekly allowance to cover the driving expense. But as the cost of cars, gas, and repairs rose over the next twenty years, the allowance stayed the same, effectively leading to a pay cut. Dad had gone from driving a midsize Oldsmobile sedan to a beat-up Datsun.

Trying to be helpful, I went to the library and looked up the new Dodge he was considering in *Consumer Reports*. I researched how the car performed in terms of safety and reliability, based on extensive testing by engineers and ratings from thousands of people who owned the same car. I dropped by Mason's, the bar where he stopped off most days for an after-work beer, and proudly reported my findings. He said, "That's fine, son," and went on to tell me that his friend Jim used to own the same kind of car, and it ran for two hundred thousand miles. I started to explain my newfound wisdom on why the ratings of thousands of users are more reliable than a single anecdote, but his eyes lost interest. I could feel the distance between us growing. I stopped talking and sat down at the bar and joined him for a beer.

Too often, highly educated people assume that less-educated people who disagree with them are simply not as smart. But assuming that people who disagree with you are unintelligent is one of the laziest ways that the psychological immune system maintains a sense of superiority. In my experience, that thought is a sign that you are fooling yourself. Education changes the way people make sense of the world in lots of ways, but its effects are not simple or obvious.

The correlation between higher education and liberal politics is just that—a correlation. It turns out that a chunk of that association is not caused by education at all. Instead, liberal-leaning families send their kids to college at a higher rate than conservative families. After college, liberal graduates are more likely to pursue an advanced degree. So some of the correlation between education and politics is really a sorting effect, as liberal people spend more time in higher education.

So what happens once people are in college? Contrary to the widespread view that universities indoctrinate students with liberal ideologies, research shows that students do not generally become more liberal in their policy views during their years in school. College students and graduates certainly hold more liberal policy opinions than those who have not gone to college, but they show up for college already holding those views.

This might seem hard to believe, given how prominent the narrative of liberal indoctrination is. To be sure, faculty are more liberal than the general population, with about three liberals for every conservative professor on average, and a ratio of more than five to one at elite schools. One study tracked sixty-eight hundred students in thirty-eight colleges and universities that varied a lot in how liberal the faculty were. The students rated themselves on a scale from liberal to conservative in their first year of college and again in their fourth year. Overall, students did not become more liberal or conservative over time. They started as somewhat liberal on average, and they finished somewhat liberal. The political leanings of the faculty didn't make any difference. Regardless of how liberal the faculty were, students tended to stay the same.

It turns out that political identities are like accents: they drift toward your peer group, not your teachers. One study tracked students across their first year of college and took advantage of the fact that at some colleges roommates are assigned by a random allocation. That turns the roommate lottery into a natural experiment to test whether roommates cause shifts in political views. Sure enough, the study found that students assigned to a more liberal roommate became slightly more liberal, and those assigned a more conservative roommate became a bit more conservative. Students on the whole did not become more liberal or conservative across their first year, because for every student paired with someone more liberal there was also a student paired with someone more conservative. The effects of roommates canceled out. Still, the study is revealing for showing the importance of peer groups as young people form their political identities.

The studies just described looked at general measures of how liberal or conservative students rated themselves to be. But those might not be the most important measures to look at, because as we have seen, politics is more about group identities than abstract ideologies. Studies that looked at the effects of education on group-based identities and attitudes tell quite a different story. Scores of studies have found that college students and college graduates score much lower on measures of racial and gender bias than those without a college education. But most of those studies can't distinguish whether college causes shifts in those views, or whether people who are lower on those measures are more likely to go to college. A few studies over the last several years, however, have examined pairs of siblings to sort out cause and effect. They tracked pairs in which one sibling went to college and the other did not. Siblings from the same household would each be influenced by family background characteristics in similar ways. So the sibling who does not go to college can serve as a control group to compare against the sibling who enrolled.

What they found is that causality works in both directions. More liberal individuals are indeed more likely to attend college. But once in college, those students go on to become more aware of systemic racism, less likely to see racial inequality as a result of Black people's failings, and more likely to support gender equality, compared to their siblings. Although college does not appear to make students rate themselves as more liberal in general, it does make them more concerned about group-based inequalities, which, as we have seen, are the main driving forces behind political identities.

These study results resonate with my experience as a college student. I could not have identified the politics of most of my professors, and I would not have tried to mold my views to theirs in any case. I cared a lot about what my friends thought, but we did not talk much about politics. It was the books I read that shaped my worldview more than anything else, but not in a way that had a direct bearing on political issues. I remember reading Locke and Mill and finding them so much more persuasive than Burke, with his defense of the monarchy and the Church. But that had no bearing on my attitudes toward Bill Clinton or Bob Dole.

It was literature classes that made the first difference for me. It was Faulkner's grim, funny, and sympathetic portrayal of proud and ignorant White southerners refusing to change with the rest of the world. It was seeing the small-town South through the eyes of Scout in *To Kill a Mockingbird*. And it was sympathizing with a young Black girl in Toni Morrison's *The Bluest Eye*, a book that haunted me long after I read it. Reading fiction was an exercise in empathy that helped me realize that no one is wrong or evil from their own point of view. So understanding people means understanding their point of view.

I had an American history class in college, but I don't remember much from it. It was the kind of class that asks students to memorize names and dates and great battles. Later, in graduate school and beyond, I would start to read about the history of slavery and about the way defeated Confederates settled in for a war of attrition and resistance during the Reconstruction period. I read, mostly outside of classes, about the redlining that created today's racially segregated cities. And this is how I first learned that one generation's inequality of outcomes becomes the next generation's inequality of opportunity.

For me, like most college students, it was not learning about political science or economics or even philosophy that shaped my political worldview. It was learning about social identities, group hierarchies, and their histories that made the difference. But applying those lessons about the past to understand the present also required the kind of counterintuitive analytic thinking that I trained on Linda the bank teller.

When most people think about racial disparities, they think about individuals. They might look at a person panhandling and think, like I once did, that they should just get a job. When young children are asked to explain why good events happen to some people and bad events happen to others, they tend to say that the lucky person is better in some way. They assumed that they behaved better or they were nicer, or they worked harder. As children grow older, they develop more sophisticated ways of thinking about inequalities. Understanding that the lives of individuals reflect larger histories and systems requires education and practice with abstract analytical thinking.

The preference of wealthy people for Republicans is not new. But the tension of income and education pulling in opposite directions is very new. In fact, it can be traced largely to the election of Barack Obama followed by Donald Trump. These elections signaled that race was the single largest dividing line between Democrats and Republicans. College-educated people started aligning with Democrats, and people without college educations backed Republicans.

Well, not all people. The diploma divide is driven entirely by White Americans. Non-White Americans favor Democrats by a similar margin regardless of their education level.

So the diploma divide comes down to a racial divide among White voters. The voting differences between highly educated and less-educated White people can now be fully accounted for by differences in views of racial inequality. Recall the "racial resentment" questions from chapter 4 that asked about whether racial inequality is due to discrimination or a lack of effort among Black people. When researchers statistically control for those racial attitudes, the diploma divide among White voters disappears. That is to say, if you selected a sample of voters who all believed that inequality is mainly about discrimination, they would vote overwhelmingly for Democrats, regardless of their education level. And if you selected a group who believed inequality is mainly about a lack of effort, they would vote overwhelmingly Republican—the PhDs and the high school dropouts alike.

Research by psychologist Phia Salter shows that the less factual information people know about the history of segregation and discrimination, the less they believe that today's racial inequalities are due to structural factors, and the more they believe they are due to personal failings. Teaching students about history, in contrast, increases their recognition of structural barriers. The lack of historical knowledge is not purely out of ignorance, however. When researchers cued people to feel especially close to their in-groups, they suddenly could not remember as many historical instances when their group had been violent toward other groups. In other words, it's not only that ignorance of history shapes people's current beliefs about groups. It's that people's group-based emotions can make people less able to recall history. Like vacationers who misremember how much they enjoyed their vacations, people tend to misremember history to fit their current desires.

The connection between education and political identity is making higher education a new political battleground. When people with little education disagree with highly educated people, they don't think of themselves as less knowledgeable or misinformed. That would be inconsistent with their psychological bottom line. Instead, they embrace the narrative that coastal elites have hijacked the country and the culture. They have stolen the country from ordinary people, from "real" Americans.

You can see the psychological immune system at work in the spate of laws that have been passed by Republican-controlled state legislatures banning schools from teaching about history, slavery, and race. These laws seem particularly focused on preventing students from being taught that history continues to influence the present. A Tennessee law, for example, prohibits teaching that "this state or the United States is fundamentally or irredeemably racist or sexist." It bans the idea that "a meritocracy is inherently racist or sexist, or designed by a particular race or sex to oppress members of another race or sex." It prohibits teaching that "an individual, by virtue of the individual's race or sex, is inherently privileged, racist, sexist, or oppressive, whether consciously or subconsciously," and that, "an individual, by virtue of the individual's race or sex, bears responsibility for actions committed in the past by other members of the same race or sex."

In my own North Carolina, House Bill 324, passed in 2021 but vetoed by the Democratic governor, declared that "public school units shall not promote that an individual, solely by virtue of his or her race or sex, bears responsibility for actions committed in the past by other members of the same race or sex."

These prohibitions seem designed to protect White people's psychological bottom line that they are good and reasonable, and their groups are too. Although there has been no evidence that public school teachers were actually teaching children that they should feel anything "solely by virtue of his or her race or sex," the defensiveness is obvious. You can almost hear the echoes of previous generations' defense of slavery and the defense of Jim Crow after that. "We didn't create racial inequalities, we just inherited them. Our generation bears no responsibility!" In states with such laws, the material covered in this book would likely be illegal in the classroom. At the very least, many teachers would be afraid to cover it for fear they would be punished.

I doubt these laws will have any impact in slowing the liberalizing effect of education when it comes to race, sex, and other social-group attitudes. College students don't become more aware of systemic racism because a teacher tells them that they "bear responsibility" for slavery "solely because of their race," or any other such cartoonish claims. The change in perspective results from a thousand smaller lessons and social interactions that happen daily on college campuses. You simply can't spend four years reading novels by Toni Morrison and history by Eric Foner and philosophy by Thomas Nagel without having your worldview challenged and broadened. When students do that, they don't necessarily come to view themselves as more liberal. But the worldview of a Trump supporter comes to feel much more alien.

The worldviews of less-educated family members become more alien too. This creates a heart-wrenching tension for conservative parents. They know that sending their children to college is the best way to secure a middle-class life for them. But they also know the full college experience will change them. A relative once told me she was not saving a college fund for her kids. "They come back . . ." She paused, regarding me for a minute. "They come back atheists. And what good is money in this world compared to an eternity in hellfire?" Eternity in hellfire is hard to argue with. Where to even begin? I suspect that sense of foreignness was behind Dad's admonishment, when I was about to leave for college, not to become a goddamned long-haired hippie. And the truth is, he was right. I no longer have the long hair. But I will always be a little distant, a little alien. I even have a foreign accent.

SIX

COUNTRY PEOPLE

And if the world went to hell in a handbasket—
as it seemed to be doing—you could say good-bye
to everyone and retreat to your land,
hunkering down and living off it.

—JEANNETTE WALLS

I can't remember the first time I shot a shotgun any more than I can remember the first time I ate with a fork. They were such commonplace implements that they were not very memorable. I do recall, however, the first time I shot a pistol. We were visiting Dad's brother Matthew. Matthew lived alone in a hollowed-out school bus wedged between the trees down an old dirt road. With the seats removed, it was more spacious than you might imagine. Where the driver's seat had been, there was a coal stove. A few yards outside the bus was an outhouse. All these years later and he was still living the way he and Dad were raised.

It was the first time I had been to Matthew's place, and I thought it was the coolest thing I'd ever seen. I was seven or eight years old. He showed me how he pumped the handle on an old pitcher pump to draw his water and how he built the coal fire. He took me to the chicken coop to get some eggs, and then we scrambled them on the coal stove. My favorite television show in those days was *Grizzly Adams*, about a man who fled to the wilderness because he was wrongfully accused of murder. He built his own cabin, befriended a bear, and learned to live off the land. Uncle Matthew impressed me as a real-life Grizzly Adams. It never occurred to me back then to wonder what he was running from.

After breakfast, Matthew asked me if I wanted to shoot a pistol. It was a very old-looking revolver. He showed me how to remove the safety, how to hold the gun, how to aim and smoothly squeeze the trigger without pulling the gun to the side. He set up a row of empty beer cans on a tree stump for me to knock down. He warned me that the gun would recoil and that I should make sure the gun went up and over my head, but my arms were not strong enough, and I still hit myself in the forehead the first time. Matthew and Dad tried not to laugh. I eventually got the hang of it, and I still remember the thrill of pulling the trigger and sending a beer can flying.

My family has a complicated relationship with guns. Dad shot my brother Jason once, and he never heard the end of it. Dad was shooting tin cans in the backyard for target practice. When you are drawing a bead on a Budweiser can thirty feet away, you can't see what's happening in the periphery. That's when Jason came riding his bike through the yard. The bullet went in the side of his calf and came out in his shoe. Dad stopped shooting pistols in the backyard after that. Yet, several years later, we were still shooting cans at Uncle Matthew's place. Brad contacted the siblings a while back to see if we wanted to chip in on a pair of pearl-handled pistols as a Christmas present for Dad. He hadn't had a pistol, Brad said, since

Mom made him get rid of the one he shot Jason with. Dad is eighty now and doesn't see so well, so I declined to contribute.

My friends and I all had BB guns before we got real ones. We would have BB gun wars, fighting running battles through the woods and fields around my house. We thought we were being careful, because we dressed in thick coveralls. We wore safety goggles over our eyes and ski masks over our faces. I soon found out that a ski mask won't stop a BB. My friend Steve shot me in the forehead, just above my goggles. I didn't dare tell my parents, so I squeezed it on both sides to pop out the BB and we bandaged it ourselves.

On my sixteenth birthday I graduated from a BB gun to a 16-gauge shotgun. Not long afterward, Dad and Jason took me rabbit hunting in the fields behind our house, which lay fallow after the fall harvest. They showed me how to walk abreast of one another so that no one is in anyone else's line of fire. We walked slowly through the fields, our boots brushing against the grass and weeds, trying to "walk up" a rabbit. We eventually flushed one out, and I felt a rush of adrenaline as Jason urged me to take the shot. But I hesitated, and my shot missed. Jason took a shot, but by that time it was too far away. We didn't take any rabbits that day, but I felt I had been initiated into a new club: Men Who Hunt.

I kept thinking about our hunt, and a couple of weeks later I went again on my own. It was a gray December day. The leaves were all down, the trees looked black, and the field was covered in pale grass. Everything looked almost black and white. Grass rustled at my feet, and a white tail bounded through the grass ahead of me. I raised the shotgun, aimed, and fired. The tail rose up, and the rabbit tumbled, its back legs flipping over its head. I ran over to where it lay, and as I stared down at the dying rabbit, all the excitement drained away. I just felt sad. I didn't want to skin the rabbit or eat it anymore. But the only thing that felt worse than that was to waste the rabbit's life for no purpose. So I skinned and field dressed it like I'd been taught, feeling sick to my stomach, and took it home. Mom coated the meat in flour and salt and pepper and fried it like chicken, and I forced myself to eat it. I never went hunting again.

As might be expected based on the psychological immune system, gun owners have different beliefs about the meaning and consequences of guns compared to those who don't own a gun. Gun owners underestimate the risks. Studies show that accidental shootings or homicides are many times more common than intentional uses of guns for self-defense. And the easier it is to get a gun in a state or country, the higher the gun violence rates are. But gun owners rarely think an accidental shooting will happen in their house. They only imagine using the gun on its intended target. And so, most gun owners believe that guns reduce violence rather than increase it. Most gun owners were born into gun-owning families and communities. Like me, they became familiar and comfortable with them at a young age. The relationship with guns is more about feelings than facts. Gun owners consider their right to have a gun as fundamental to their freedom, nearly on par with freedom of speech, freedom of religion, and the right to vote. For people who don't own guns, it is nowhere near as important as those other rights.

The most common reason gun owners give for owning a gun is "protection," followed by hunting. But what "protection" means also differs a lot between the country and the city. I grew up understanding that the Second Amendment exists so that citizens can fight and overthrow the government if it becomes tyrannical. I don't recall talking about it with parents or teachers. It was just common knowledge. That interpretation of the Second Amendment is known by legal scholars as the "insurrectionist theory" of the Second Amendment. It was long a fringe position of the far right, but in recent years it has become a mainstream view among Republicans.

Where I grew up, it was just one part of a larger survivalist culture. We had a wood-burning stove in the half-built-in carport. We used it on cold winter nights to help reduce the electricity bill. But the larger reason was that one day there might be no electricity at all. My family went hunting and fishing for recreation, I suppose. But the deeper reason was that we needed to be able to feed ourselves in case everything went to hell. I used birthday money to buy a series of "survival knives," large Bowie knives with a hollowed-out handle. Inside the handle was stuffed with survival gear, like a roll of fishing line and hooks, and a flint and striker for starting fires. Life was uncertain and precarious, filled with a general feeling that everything might fall apart any day now. Rich people looked for security in insurance and retirement funds. Those things require a lot of trust that society will still exist, that institutions like banks will still exist. But our insurance was the woods, survival knives, and guns.

Guns are just one marker of a deeper divide between urban and rural places. It is not hard to find other markers. The kinds of businesses in a place say a lot about the people who live there. Voters living within ten miles of a Whole Foods, Lululemon, or an Apple Store voted Democratic by a 30-point margin in 2016. Those living close to a Cracker Barrel, Bass Pro Shop, or Hobby Lobby voted Republican by 10 percentage points. And those living too far out to be near any chain stores voted Republican by more than 20 points.

Other choices people make about how to spend their money reveal a lot about the differences between the city and the country. Researchers from Stanford University counted the number of pickup trucks and sedans in neighborhoods across the country. Places where trucks outnumbered cars voted more than 80 percent Republican, whereas those with more sedans than trucks voted overwhelmingly Democratic.

Retail stores and pickup trucks are surface markers that advertise what kind of place we are in, but they are not what actually drives the differences between places. What deeper differences, then, do they signify? And why is it that, across many parts of the world, cities tend toward more liberal thought and the countryside is more conservative?

The strongest factor separating the politics of city people and country people isn't a feature of the land or the buildings or anything about the physical places themselves. It is population density that creates the divide. In the 2020 election, for example, the densest counties voted for Joe Biden more than 80 percent, while the least dense voted for Donald Trump by a similar margin. These trends have been strengthening each election cycle since the 1960s. But the source of this density divide goes back much further.

If the path of southern conservatives was paved in chalk, the path of liberal city dwellers was hammered in steel. As political scientist Jonathan Rodden has pointed out, a map of nineteenth-century railroad connections looks very similar to a map of Democratic voters today. Early U.S. cities were founded based on their proximity to water. Port cities like New York and New Orleans and river cities like St. Louis and Cincinnati got an early head start. But most cities that had a port didn't have good river connections to the rest of the country, and those that had rivers didn't have ports. Coastal cities like Boston, Charleston, and Baltimore became pioneers in building railroads to extend their trade to the interior of the country. The Baltimore and Ohio Railroad led the way, building a track heading out of Baltimore westward, toward the Ohio River, in 1827. At the time the building started, they did not know where exactly they would connect to the river. But by 1852, the B&O reached the Ohio at Wheeling, West Virginia.

By the mid-1800s, railroads were sprouting up all over the eastern United States, connecting cities to rivers, to ports, and to one another. Cities connected by railroad networks grew and prospered and became more attractive destinations for yet more rail lines. Midwestern cities like Chicago and Kansas City became thriving industrial centers. And when the transcontinental railroad was completed in 1869, San Francisco and Los Angeles began to grow.

These well-connected industrial centers sparked a massive wave of urbanization that continues today. In 1500, more than 90 percent of the world's population lived in rural areas. That barely changed at all for three centuries, and in 1800 still only 6 percent of Americans lived in cities. But then, drawn by factories, people started moving from the countryside into cities at an astonishing pace. By 1950, 64 percent of Americans lived in cities, and today that figure is 82 percent. By 2050, around 90 percent of Americans will live in cities.

The factories offered more money than most people made on the farm, but the conditions were horrific. Workdays were often between twelve and sixteen hours long, sometimes with no breaks for meals. Women and children as young as five years old made up

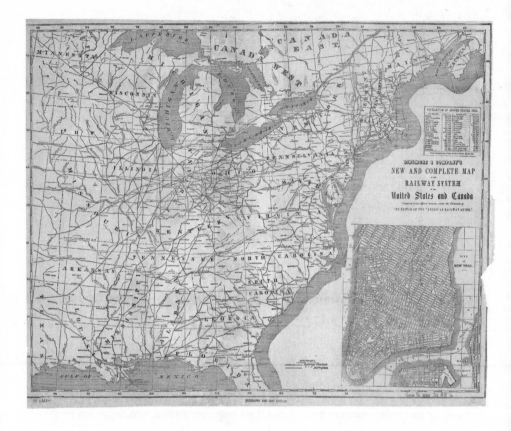

Figure 3.
Dinsmore & Company's new and complete map of the railway
system of the United States and Canada, 1850.
Curran Dinsmore, Library of Congress Geography and
Map Division, Washington, D.C.

the majority of the workers. Factory bosses used children's small
hands to reach inside the whirring machines, and their small bodies to climb inside them when needed. We do not have good data
on child mortality rates, but narrative accounts suggest that children were maimed and killed in atrocious numbers.

This was the setting in which the labor movement was born.
Although trade unions had existed long before that time, they
were small and disconnected. The American Federation of Labor

brought them together in 1886 for more coordinated collective action. The unions began staging larger strikes and demanding better pay, shorter hours, and safer working conditions. Strikes were often bloody affairs. Workers did not have legal protections for striking, and the police or National Guard troops were often called in to break up the strikes and force people back to work. In other cases, private security companies did the same job. Sometimes it was the guards or police who fired on the striking workers. Other times the workers fired first on the guards. It was not until Franklin Roosevelt passed New Deal–era legislation to protect labor unions that the violence began to subside. The laws included federal rules allowing unions to organize and established a labor relations board to enforce the prolabor provisions and mediate disputes peacefully. The Democratic Party became a workers' party allied with unions in the industrialized cities of the North, while in the rural South, it remained organized around White supremacy.

The tradition of labor unions in industrialized cities got the rural/urban divide started, but it does not explain why the divide has not only persisted but continued to grow over the last fifty years. Labor unions have shrunk during that period. Fifty years ago, about a third of the U.S. workforce was unionized, but only one in ten people belongs to a union today. The globalized economy means that the world's manufacturing centers are no longer in northern U.S. cities, having been outsourced to regions with cheaper labor. So the manufacturing and labor movements that initiated the divide between cities and countryside are unlikely to explain today's growing divisions.

Around 1900, the workers in northern factories were a mix of poor White Americans and immigrants, mostly from Ireland and eastern Europe. Then the First World War erupted. Immigration slowed to a trickle, as the United States began passing a series of laws to restrict immigration. When the U.S. joined the war, the soldiers it sent came from the same working-class groups who had powered the factories. Together, the war and stalled immigration led to labor shortages in northern cities.

So factory owners turned to another source of cheap labor: Black southerners. Northern business owners sent "recruiters" to the South to offer Black sharecroppers and farmers jobs in northern factories. It was risky business. Both the Black workers and the recruiters faced intimidation and violence by White landowners. But word soon spread from the tobacco farms in Kentucky to the cotton plantations in Mississippi that a new option had appeared. Not only could Black southerners make better money, but they could also escape the constant threat of violence and the daily indignities of the Jim Crow South.

The Great Migration had begun. Between 1910 and 1970, nearly six million Black Americans migrated, largely from southern farms to northern cities. At the beginning of the Great Migration, 90 percent of Black Americans lived in the South. But by the end, nearly half lived outside the South.

The Great Migration transformed northern cities. Historians have argued that the concentration of Black Americans in cities contributed, for example, to the Harlem Renaissance and the development of the civil rights movement. At the same time, White backlash to growing Black populations led to new barriers for Black Americans in the North. White authorities responded to the growing Black populations by segregating neighborhoods and schools. Restrictive covenants kept Black families in Black-only areas of cities. Federal housing policies known as redlining prevented Black residents from obtaining mortgages, limiting their ability to

build wealth. Black workers were barred in many places from join-
ing labor unions and were relegated to low-wage work.

As Black families moved in, White families began leaving
urban neighborhoods for fast-growing suburbs. These changes
gave rise to the organization of cities that is common today, with a
racially diverse inner core surrounded by less diverse suburbs. Today, we take for granted that cities are racially diverse—to the point
that "urban" is sometimes used as a euphemism for Black. But the
racial diversity of cities is a direct result of the Great Migration, in
which Black Americans uprooted themselves from their southern
farms in search of "the warmth of other suns," in Richard Wright's
memorable phrase.

All this internal migration created cities that really are very diverse. The U.S. population as a whole is 58 percent White, 19 percent Black, 12 percent Hispanic, and 6 percent Asian according to
the 2020 census. But the fifty largest cities have populations that
are 36 percent White, 30 percent Black, 19 percent Hispanic, and 10
percent Asian. These racial-group demographics go a long way to
explaining the political gaps between urban and rural places, as
Black, Hispanic, and Asian people are much more likely to vote
Democratic and White people are more likely to vote Republican,
for all the identity-related reasons we explored earlier.

There is another reason city dwellers are different, however:
they are much more educated than country people. To understand
why, we have to first understand that cities behave in fascinating
ways. Nearly everything about them is not linear but exponential.
At the most basic, take the population size of different cities. If
you lined up U.S. cities from the smallest to the largest, you might
expect the population size to increase a little at each step. But what
really happens is that you have many thousands of small towns

with populations below ten thousand people. Then there are about two thousand midsize cities between ten thousand and a million people. And then there are only a handful of giant cities with populations in the millions.

Within cities, the number of potential social connections increases exponentially with population size. For example, in a town of only ten people, if each person has a potential connection to each other person, then there are one hundred potential connections. In a town of one hundred people, there are ten thousand potential connections. And in a town of one hundred thousand, there are ten billion potential connections. Not every person knows every other person, of course. But the potential to make some kind of connection with another person quickly becomes vast, even in a city of moderate size.

The enormous connectivity of cities explains why they are the engines of innovation. The most innovative companies flock to urban areas because of what economist Enrico Moretti calls the "social multiplier." When businesses become large and productive, they need large teams of people with a variety of expertise. The larger the city, the easier it is for a tech company to find engineers, but also salespeople and graphic designers. The denser the population, the easier it is for a pharmaceutical company to hire not only scientists but also managers and accountants. The more universities, labs, book clubs, bars, and informal social circles there are, the more likely someone is to have a bright idea. These dynamics create a feedback loop in which the most innovative places become more prosperous, attract more diverse and skilled workers, and hence become even more innovative.

This innovation feedback loop is concentrated almost entirely in cities. Because of the social multiplier, the denser a population is, the more patents per person an area creates. In the United States, just twenty-three cities make up half of the nation's economic output. And six of the largest cities make up a quarter of the whole economy. The concentration of economic productivity means that cities attract a much more skilled and educated workforce than the countryside. And as we have seen, the more educated a person is, the more likely they are to be liberal.

The concentration of Democrats in cities means that they tend to be underrepresented in the Senate and in the Electoral College, which give a lot of weight to rural states with low populations. And it makes Democrats especially vulnerable to gerrymandering. When state legislators carve up state maps into congressional districts, they can pack together millions of Democrats in a single urban district, while spreading out a few thousand Republicans across lots of rural districts.

The growing concentration of liberals in cities and conservatives in the countryside gives the impression that Americans in recent decades have been moving to be near other like-minded people—an idea known as the Big Sort. However, one element of this theory does not add up. There is not much evidence that people are actually picking up and moving to more politically similar places.

In the most comprehensive study on this question, political scientist Jonathan Mummolo tracked millions of people's moves and compared the political leanings of the places they moved from to the political leanings of the new destination. There was simply no evidence that they sorted themselves based on politics. For one thing, people don't move often enough or far enough to account for the growing urban/rural divide. When people change houses, it is usually within the same town or city. And when they change towns, they usually move to another town nearby that is similar to where they came from.

The study found that people rarely move to a very different place. And when they did, the most common reason was for work. In most cases, they had little choice in the location. When the researchers looked at the particular neighborhoods they moved to, the biggest factors shaping their decisions were the quality of schools and affordability of home prices. In most parts of the United States, school funding is based on property taxes, so school quality is tied to home prices. Most families try to move to the best school district that their housing budget can afford. Participants in this study did indicate that they would *like* to move near politically like-minded people. But when it came to actually making the move, it was work, schools, and home prices that drove decisions.

So how are cities becoming more liberal and rural areas becoming more conservative if people are not moving to like-minded places? Part of the answer comes from research by psychologist Markus Jokela, who tracked a large sample of young adults through their school years and afterward. He found that college graduates were much more likely to move to cities, while those who didn't go to college were more likely to stay in the (mostly rural) areas where they were born. This sorting was driven by people in their twenties and thirties. So what seems to be inconsistent findings between Mummolo's study and this one most likely turns out to be the different ages of the populations. People with established homes and families are not uprooting themselves to move to a more politically congenial place. Their moves are constrained by jobs, schools, and home prices. But young people graduating from college and establishing their own homes and jobs for the first time are moving selectively. Each year, around four million new college graduates throw their mortarboards into the air. And when the celebrations are over, they pack up and move, more often than not to a major city.

The same factors that led cities to be industrial hubs in the nineteenth and twentieth centuries have led them to be technology and innovation hubs today. Those high-tech and knowledge-based industries require educated workers, which draws more educated people to cities. So to the extent that political differences are driven by demographics, the urban/rural divide is not really about cities and countryside at all. Most of the divide is driven by race and education. There are simply more White people without higher education in rural areas. And there are more non-White people and highly educated people in urban ones.

While college graduates are busy moving to bright job prospects and tiny apartments, high school graduates are staying put, getting jobs in or near their hometowns. Those small towns have populations that are stagnant or shrinking and tend to have little industry or technical innovation. While nineteenth-century railroad tracks blazed the urban trail for college graduates, a very different history was unfolding in the open fields and pastures of the countryside.

Farming and ranching communities need a lot of land. That means that a family raising cattle, herding sheep, or settling the frontier probably lived a long way from their neighbors, and even farther from a town. When those communities were settled, it was a major obstacle to ride into town to get supplies. And if there was a problem, getting a doctor or a county sheriff was difficult or impossible.

Living in remote places led to what researchers call a "culture of honor." The idea is that people living in remote or rugged areas had to learn to solve problems and settle disputes for themselves. They created a culture of self-reliance and individualism as a way to deal with the day-to-day problems they faced. Neighbors would help neighbors, but people had little regard for the laws, norms, or promises of people in faraway cities. They had even less regard for the government in Washington, D.C., which passed laws but could not enforce them out on the frontier. Each family was expected to provide for themselves. Disconnected from newspapers and mail, rural communities often lost touch with the broader culture and became insular. You can see this trend in historical records of baby names. Cut off from a single mainstream culture, names out West grew more and more idiosyncratic over time. Back east, parents kept naming their children the same common names: John and William were the most common for boys, Mary and Anna for girls. But on the frontier, curious and unusual names began to proliferate. The frontier was full of people called Ambrose, Elihu, Fern, and Zella.

One of the most distinctive features of the culture of honor is the high rate of violence. Unable to appeal to local law enforcement, rural people developed informal ways to enforce their own rules. On the one hand, this meant that people went out of their way to avoid giving offense, which may have given rise to the reputation of rural areas and especially the South for politeness. On the other hand, it meant that if offense was given, the consequences were dire. If you can't call the police to protect yourself and your family, the next best thing is to develop a reputation as someone who is not to be trifled with. And the only way to make that reputation credible is to actually demonstrate from time to time that you are willing and able to be violent. The rugged individualism of rural areas does not encourage just any kind of violence, but specifically violence aimed at defending yourself, your family, and your reputation—that is, your honor.

Psychologists Dov Cohen and Richard Nisbett tested this idea in a famous experiment. The study took place at the University of Michigan. The participants were undergraduate men, some of whom were raised in southern states and others who were raised in northern states. Participants were tested one at a time. They started the study in one lab room and then were asked to go down the hall to another room to finish up. In the hallway was an actor working as part of the study. As the participant walked by, the actor bumped him with his shoulder. Then, as if it were the participant's fault, the actor said under his breath, "Asshole."

Southerners became more upset by this provocation than northerners did. They expressed more anger and aggression in their body language. When the researchers analyzed their hormones, they had elevated cortisol and testosterone, suggesting a stress response. In one version of the study, after the participant passed the actor in the hall, the hallway narrowed to a stretch that was wide enough for only one person. The researchers planted a second actor there. He was six feet three and weighed two hundred and fifty pounds. He walked through the narrow hallway just as the research participant was passing through, creating a game of chicken, to see how close the participant would get before he yielded. In a control condition where the participant was not bumped or insulted, the southerners were more polite than the northerners, yielding especially early to let the actor pass by. But in the condition where they were provoked, southerners were more aggressive than the northerners, refusing to give way until the last second.

It's hard, for me at least, not to feel bad for these insulted southerners coping with an unwinnable confrontation. The culture of honor rings true to my experience. The immediate context of my childhood—a Catholic school—could not be further from the Wild West mentality. We operated by rules and laws. But even within that strict regiment, there was a clear expectation that boys should learn to stand up for themselves. We were constantly getting into scuffles with brothers and friends who skirted the line between playing and fighting. But I was in only two real fights. The first was on the playground in grade school. A kid named Matthew and I started scuffling over a kickball, and it escalated into wrestling and then flying fists. It was a blur of punches and playground dirt and pulled shirttails that lasted only a few seconds before teachers pulled us apart. I thought we would be in trouble, but the teachers took a "boys will be boys" approach. If they told my parents, I never heard about it. Matthew and I made up and forgot about it the next day.

The second fight was in high school. It was also, improbably, with a boy named Matthew. He was a bully, older and bigger than me. He had no reason to pick on me, in particular, that day. I just happened to be the one in front of him as we boarded the school bus that afternoon. He tried to push me out of his way and into a seat on the side. If I had just allowed myself to be pushed into the seat, it would have been over with, at least for the day. But I resisted, held on to the seat, and stood up straight and faced him. That pissed him off. He slapped me in the face, and I slapped him right back. Then there was a whirl of hands and fists and forearms until the bus driver, a tough old man with burn scars on his face, pulled us apart.

I didn't "win" that fight, but neither did he, and that was the point. Facing off with him was a reflex, drilled into me by the many times my parents and other people had said that if you let a bully push you around they will just come back for more after that. Their advice was right in this case. No parents or teachers were called. He picked on someone else the next week. It wasn't that he was afraid of me, so much as that picking on me would now be a hassle, and it was easier to move on to the next guy. I was at least an inconvenient person to trifle with.

The culture of honor is not just about southerners being violent. The logic applies anytime people are isolated and have to enforce norms for themselves rather than appeal to a centralized authority. Frontier regions face these same conditions. As American settlers spread west from the original thirteen colonies, nearly all of the country was considered "the frontier" at one time or another. But they remained frontier regions for different lengths of time. Around 1800, the frontier meant Ohio, Kentucky, and Tennessee. Around 1830, it roughly lined up with the Mississippi River. And by 1860, it included Kansas, Nebraska, the Dakotas, and Texas. Economist Samuel Bazzi used census records of population counts to draw the boundaries of the frontier throughout the eighteenth and nineteenth centuries. Certain areas of the Midwest, the Great Plains, and Texas were frontier country for much longer than most other parts of the country.

Based on this data, Bazzi found that the total amount of time that a county spent as frontier predicted the political leanings of people living there today. Areas that spent a lot of time as frontier are now more likely to vote Republican. Residents in those areas were more supportive of cutting government spending to help the poor on education, and more opposed to government intervention in general. They were more likely to oppose Obamacare, oppose raising the minimum wage, and oppose regulations on guns and carbon emissions. In short, the rugged individualism required by frontier life can be seen in political cultures today. Residents of those areas (who are still overwhelmingly White) still believe people should take care of themselves and don't want the government involved in helping poor or marginalized people.

The railroads that formed cities and the wagon trails that created much of the western parts of the country set up pressures that are still at work today. Social scientists have theorized that something about living in a city makes people more liberal. Perhaps having to get along with millions of people in a dense city makes people realize the importance of government-funded common goods, from streets and subway systems to well-functioning garbage and sanitation systems. Or perhaps the intense interconnectedness of living in a diverse city leads to reduced prejudice and ethnocentrism. Or maybe just being around other liberals makes city dwellers more liberal, while being around other conservatives makes country people more conservative. These theories seem plausible, but it is hard to find good data in support of them.

The jury is still out on whether living in a city or rural area causes changes in people's political views. But there is overwhelming evidence that urban and rural areas have attracted different groups of people. Whether it was our ancestors who immigrated to work in factories or to settle the frontier, or college graduates moving to the cities, the populations of city and rural areas have become radically different.

I am one of those college graduates who moved to a city. When I moved to St. Louis for graduate school, I was overawed as I drove into the city and saw the skyline of tall buildings and the giant arch on the horizon. I loved being able to walk out of my apartment building and get a coffee and a bagel on the next block. I loved the light-rail system that would take me effortlessly to a Cardinals game or to the airport. There were street festivals and block parties. But more than these amenities, I loved that I had found my people.

Visiting home from St. Louis made Kentucky feel even farther away. Driving down Highway 60 past the steel mill and the coal plant and the elementary school with the detention center across the street felt like a barely remembered dream. And the memories from my childhood, like shooting pistols with Uncle Matthew at his school bus in the woods, seemed like a movie of someone else's life.

The name Matthew means "a gift from God." If I were given to mystical thinking, I might wonder whether these encounters with the pistol and the playground fight and the high school fight were sent to teach me something. Sent or not, I suppose they did teach me something. Today I can't imagine letting a seven-year-old shoot a firearm or encouraging boys to solve their problems by fighting. But in that time and place, those choices served a function. In many parts of the world, they still do.

When I was growing up, the source of tyranny that we needed guns to fight against was vague. Maybe it was "the government," but I doubt gun owners expected the Reagan administration to send troops marching into their towns. Maybe it was a Russian invasion, and people imagined themselves as resistance fighters, like in the movie *Red Dawn*. Maybe it was some natural disaster that would leave us all defending our homes and hunting to survive, *Mad Max*–style. But more likely, it was an abstract idea that sometime in the future, the world might change so much that we will need to fight some enemy who hasn't yet been envisioned.

Today the enemy seems much less abstract. During the Black Lives Matter protests that followed the murder of George Floyd in

2020, I saw relatives posting online that this is why people need guns—to protect against "the hordes." Now I regularly see posts saying that the government trying to "take our guns" would be the start of a civil war. Increasingly, the tyrannical enemies in the imaginations of the gun owners I know are simply Democrats. Another relative posted recently that people need to start farming and storing food out of fear for where the country is heading. They recommended canning at least three years of food for when "the shit hits the fan." The post ended ominously: "the fight is at our doorstep." The particular sources of threat keep changing, but those changes are mostly at the surface level. The threat that underlies them all is a changing social order, in which the groups that used to dominate society are being increasingly challenged by groups that were once powerless.

SEVEN

GOD'S PEOPLE

If God is for us, who can be against us?

—ROMANS 8:31

That afternoon, when the car skidded off the highway and plowed through our front yard, I had a hunch something much bigger was happening. Why would a driver do that in broad daylight? Come to think of it, I hadn't actually seen a driver at all. Suddenly it dawned on me. Maybe there was no driver. Maybe they had disappeared.

The book of Matthew, chapter 24, says, "There will be two men in the field; one will be taken and one will be left. Two women will be grinding at the mill; one will be taken and one will be left." The pastor in Mom's church talked about this chapter with the drama of a science-fiction movie. He seemed confident that it would happen in our lifetimes. "Imagine what it will be like," he'd say. "They'll be walking down the street and people will just vanish. Cars will crash. Airplanes are going to fall from the sky. The godless world is going to think there is some great mystery. They'll say it was aliens or spies or some great conspiracy. But we will know, it is the Lord. It is the Rapture."

The rapture, for many evangelical Christians, marks the beginning of the end-times. God will call the true believers to heaven so they do not have to endure the tribulations to come. The wicked and the unbelievers will be left behind to endure seven years of strife, during which Jesus returns to Earth and conquers his enemies. I stopped worrying about the people in that car and started worrying about a bigger problem.

Why were we left behind?

Life in a fundamentalist religious community can be frightening because you see the hand of God—and the hand of Satan—behind ordinary events. That life imbues everyday struggles with the righteousness of an epic battle between good and evil. But in the end, it is comforting, because it also comes with an assurance that God is on our side. We are the chosen people. Religion is the ultimate system for assuring us that we are good and reasonable people, and that our groups are too.

More and more, religious-group identities are lining up with political-group identities. In 2019, about 80 percent of Republicans identified as Christians, as compared to only 55 percent of Democrats. But identifying as Christian or another religion can mean many different things to people. If we look at more fine-grained distinctions, the political differences are even starker. According to 2020 exit polls, White Christians who considered themselves evangelical or born again voted for Donald Trump by a whopping 84 percent. White mainline Protestants favored Trump, but by a slimmer margin of 57 percent to 43 percent, almost identical to White Catholics. Biden, on the other hand, overwhelmingly won the votes of Black Protestants (91 percent) and the religiously unaffiliated (71 percent), as well as the catchall category of "other" religious groups not specified in the poll (64 percent).

Where does this religion divide come from? When I first started researching this question, I expected a straightforward story about the ways that children are socialized into their family's religion, and those religious groups shape what political camps they are attracted to. Religious affiliations are learned early, after all, and for many people they are fundamental guiding principles that ought to shape other belief systems. But the reality is more complicated than that. Political identities and religious identities have a sophisticated give-and-take, with each one influencing the other at key moments. To understand this dance, we have to understand how and why people come to believe—or not believe—in religions at all.

Earth is a very religious place. Studies estimate that between 80 and 85 percent of the world's population is religious. The vast majority (around 75 percent) belong to one of the four largest religions—Christians, Muslims, Hindus, and Buddhists. A lot of other smaller religions, including Judaism, Bahaism, Jainism, Sikhism, Shintoism, Taoism, and Zoroastrianism, together make up another 1 percent of the planet. There are hundreds of other religious groups (perhaps thousands, depending on how the boundaries are drawn), often considered "folk religions," among various ethnic or Indigenous groups. Together, they make up about 6 percent of the world's population.

And then there are those who don't affiliate with any religious group. According to surveys, they make up about 16 percent of the world, similar to the number of Hindus. In the United States, the religious landscape is changing fast, and the changes are driven mainly by the rapid increase in people with no religion. In 1990,

90 percent of Americans were Christian, and only 5 percent were nonreligious. As of 2021, the share of Christians has fallen to 63 percent, and those with no religious affiliation has risen to 29 percent. If current trends continue, around 2070 the nonreligious will outnumber Christians.

Not all of those who claim no religion are atheists or agnostics, however. According to Gallup, which asks "Do you believe in God?" directly in their surveys, about 17 percent of Americans say no. That is up from 11 percent in 2011, and from a steady 1 to 3 percent between the 1940s through the '60s. That kind of direct survey question might underestimate the number of atheists, though, because people often worry they will be negatively judged for saying they don't believe in God. A clever study led by psychologist Will Gervais suggests the real rate might be much higher.

Gervais's research team surveyed a sample representative of the demographics of the U.S. population but used an experiment to estimate people's beliefs indirectly. One group was given a list of several statements and were asked to indicate how many—but not which ones—were true of them. For example, some of the statements included "I am a vegetarian," "I can drive a motorcycle," and "I own a dog." Another group of respondents saw the same list of statements with one additional statement: "I do not believe in God." Respondents simply indicated the number of statements that were true for them.

From the perspective of any given respondent, this question does not reveal whether they believe in God. But from the perspective of the researchers, this simple experiment allows them to estimate how many people in the population do not believe in God. Because people are randomly assigned to one group or the other, it is unlikely that there are more vegetarians, motorcyclists, or dog owners in one group than the other, on average. The only systematic difference between the groups is that one was asked about their belief in God. Participants said that a higher percentage of items described them in the condition that included "I do not believe in God." Based on these results, Gervais and colleagues estimated the rate of atheists to be 26 percent of the population. If one in four Americans is atheist, we are already a much less religious society than most people assume.

Why do some people drift toward atheism while others feel drawn to fundamentalist or evangelical churches? Each of us, as individuals, feels that we have embarked on a unique journey full of thoughtful consideration and soul-searching. For me, the journey started in middle school. In my Catholic school, religion class was required every year. I was a straight-A student, but something started to change around seventh grade. I started getting Cs, but only in religion class.

Just before lunch we had math class, where we learned geometry and algebra. When solving geometry problems, it was drilled into our heads that we could not just look at the pictures of triangles or circles and guess the answers, because the pictures were often not drawn to scale. We had to reason through the problems to find the angle or compute the area. The teacher was right—when I tried to make intuitive guesses on quizzes I got the problems wrong. Logic and arithmetic were the only way to get through the tests.

After lunch, we had religion class. It was taught by Sister Mary, a youngish woman with thick glasses, who also taught music class and sang beautifully. Different rules applied in religion class. For example, we learned from the Catechism that "Jesus Christ possesses two natures, one divine and the other human, not confused, but united in the one person of God's Son. . . . The Incarnation is therefore the mystery of the wonderful union of the divine and human natures in the one person of the Word." I asked questions, politely, sincerely—I would have never had the gall to confront the teacher directly—about how someone can be both human and God at the same time. We had learned in math class that something cannot be both X and not-X at the same time.

"It's a mystery," she said. "Human minds cannot understand the nature of God."

"Contradiction," I wrote in my notebook. I wondered why they bothered explaining anything about the topic at all if it was impossible to understand. I longed for the clean precision of algebra.

I felt guilty for having such blasphemous thoughts. I confessed them to Father Glahn during the sacrament of reconciliation, but only in vague forms. I asked forgiveness for doubt and for uncharitable thoughts. He assigned me some Hail Marys as penance, and I was on my way. I felt lighter for a bit, having unburdened myself of my sins and doubts. But as soon as I was out the door, I wondered whether the whole reconciliation ritual was playacting.

I was not bold enough to challenge the nuns or the priest overtly in class. But in the silence and solitude of tests, my subversive thoughts were expressed. "How do we know what God is like?" read one question. The correct answer was, "Revelation through Scripture, and sacred Church Tradition." But I wrote, "We don't."

"In what degree must we accept the Bible? In what degree Tradition?" The correct answer was, "One must accept the Bible and Tradition completely and equally because both are revealed by God." I wrote, "We have to think for ourselves."

I did well on factual questions, like "Which Gospel includes the Beatitudes?" But there were enough questions about doctrine and faith that the Cs replaced the As. I thought Sister Mary might call my parents in for a parent-teacher conference. But that's not what she did. One day near the end of the school year, she pulled me aside in the hallway. She said, "You think you're smart. You think you're invincible. But mark my word, you are going to need God one day." And then she walked away. Was it a friendly word to the wise? A veiled threat? I came to realize that it was both.

In high school, we still had required religion classes, but not enough priests and nuns to teach them. There was only one priest and one or two nuns in the whole school. They wrang their hands about the decline of the priesthood. So Religion I and Religion II were taught by the men's soccer coach. He wasn't remotely qualified to teach a course on Catholicism, so class consisted of opening the Bible each day, reading it quietly at our desks, and outlining it in our notebooks until the bell rang. In Religion I we outlined the Old Testament. Religion II was the New Testament. I felt like an ancient scribe whose job was copying the Bible before the invention of the printing press.

The truth is, I loved it. I preferred quiet reading over listening to a lecture. I enjoyed puzzling through the baroque biblical language and translating it into plain English. And I loved studying the original text rather than having it summarized for me. Although I had been taught parts of the Bible hundreds of times in religion classes and in Sunday sermons, they always seemed to choose the same passages. The passages were selected for their clear and simple morals. I had heard the story of Abraham countless times. How Abraham was called by God to found a new nation, and how he dutifully obeyed every command. And then, when commanded by God to sacrifice his only son, Isaac, Abraham was willing to do the unthinkable. But God relented at the last moment, sparing Isaac and allowing Abraham to sacrifice a ram instead.

The moral in the homily was about trusting and obeying God, even when our own sense of reason and morality say otherwise. If you have faith, the priest would say, God will not let you down. The stories in the homilies had happy endings—even Hollywood endings. In the court of the wise King Solomon, the baby is never really cut in half.

But those days of silently reading and outlining the Bible opened up other kinds of stories. They were dark and violent. If they had any meaning, it was the bleak irony of a murder ballad. I read the story of Jephthah, a military commander leading the Israelites in battle against the Ammonites. He vowed to God that if he was successful in battle, he would sacrifice to God whoever came out the door of his house to greet him when he returned. As he approached the house, it was not some servant but his daughter, his only child, who came out to welcome him home. Jephthah was devastated, but he dared not break his vow. This time God issued no last-minute reprieve. So Jephthah burned his daughter to death. End of story.

Closely reading the Bible didn't make me believe more or less in any direct way. But it alerted me to how cherry-picked most people's biblical stories were. Theologians have interpreted the story of Jephthah in multiple ways. Some see it as an example of unflinching devotion to God, like the Abraham story. Others see it as a cautionary tale, in which Jephthah is a foolish man for making a careless oath to God. In my community, citing a Bible passage was a way of claiming moral authority for whatever point you want to make. The more I learned about the Bible, the more I realized how morally ambiguous much of it was. For every passage in Deuteronomy explaining how to stone a sinner to death, there was a story of Jesus saying to an angry mob, "He that is without sin among you, let him first cast a stone." It was an early hint, for me, that people used texts to rationalize whatever they already believed rather than trying to discover the truth.

Not everyone grows up in such an intense, literal-minded religious tradition. But somehow, most of the world ends up believing in some religion. From within any particular religion, it seems obvious that people believe what they believe because they are simply seeing reality. Of course, different religious groups believe opposing things, so they can't all be right. The Crucifixion and Resurrection of Jesus are central to Christianity but have no place in Buddhism. Reincarnation is critical to Hinduism but not Judaism. And none of those religions would agree with Shinto animists that all objects have souls.

The vast majority of humans believe in some religion, but they all believe such different things. This global consensus cries out for an explanation. One commonality across the world's religions is the belief in supernatural agents—beings who can think and feel and do things but who lack the corporeal body of ordinary people and animals. Gods, demons, angels, and ghosts make up an interesting set of beings, because no one can document them, yet most people believe in them.

A leading theory by cognitive scientist Justin Barrett argues that the tendency to believe in supernatural agents is a consequence of humans' exquisite sensitivity to ordinary agents. An agent is an active doer—someone or something that acts with intentions, plans, or desires. In daily life, people have to be vigilant for other agents, whether it is other people or potential predators or prey lurking in the tree line. An agent—who could help or hurt us—is relevant to us in ways that rocks and trees can't be. And so, Barrett argues, humans evolved a highly sensitive ability to detect agency in the world around us.

It is so sensitive, in fact, that we tend to perceive agency in countless inanimate patterns in the world. We see faces in electrical outlets and the grills of cars. We see bulls and archers in the constellations of stars. We see hurricanes and volcanoes and the coffee tables that stub our toes as having malevolent intent. We rarely make the opposite mistake of missing agency in a real agent. This hair-trigger perception of agency is functional because it is much more harmful to be oblivious to an agent who is there than to imagine an agent who is not. It is agents, not inanimate objects, that present the most potent opportunities and dangers.

This tendency to see agency everywhere may predispose us to believing in gods, spirits, and other supernatural agents. We see faces in the clouds. We hear voices in the wind. When we look at the awe-inspiring complexity of a colony of ants or the baffling beauty of a bird of paradise in its mating dance, it is hard for us not to see the hand of a creator. And when something unexplainable happens, like the sudden death of a loved one, we look for an invisible "who" to explain the "why."

Agency detection helps explain why belief in the supernatural, in general, is common around the world, but it doesn't reveal much about the specific content of people's beliefs. Why is Jesus the chief supernatural agent for most people in the United States, while it is Allah for most people in Saudi Arabia? In one sense, the answer is easy: people adopt the dominant religious faiths of the cultures and families in which they are raised. That simple fact explains the vast majority of people's religious beliefs around the globe. If you know a child is about to be born to a family with a particular religion, you can predict with a great deal of certainty what religion the child will adopt.

When people leave behind the religion in which they were raised, they follow a predictable path. They almost never convert from one religion to a completely different religious tradition. In the United States, fewer than 1 percent of Christians convert to Hinduism or Islam or Judaism. And a similar small number convert from other religions to Christianity. When people change religions, they almost always take one of two routes. They either switch to a different denomination within the same religious tradition, or they leave religion behind altogether.

Political scientist Michele Margolis studied how religious and political identities change across the lifespan and found that both change in strikingly regular ways. Childhood is a time of religious socialization. Parents take great care to expose children to their own religious traditions, teachings, and churches. As a result, children overwhelmingly identify with whatever religion their parents are. But this all changes in adolescence. The teenage and young adult years are the least religious years of most people's lives. Church attendance for eighteen- to twenty-five-year-olds plummets to around 15 percent. The percentage of people identifying as nonreligious spikes during this period. This phase is not about the parents; it's about the young people sorting out their lives. Young adults distance themselves from their parents' religion at similar rates whether they are from a highly devout family or not, and whether they are close to their parents or not. It is a time of gaining independence and establishing their own social circles and beliefs.

Most young adults drift away from religion, but that is not the end of the story. Many of them will return by their thirties or forties. They are especially likely to return to their religious roots if they marry, have children, or both. Just as it was important to their parents to socialize them into the family religion, now they begin to find it important to include their own children. Church provides young families a source of community and social support in addition to transmitting shared values. Parenthood even makes atheists more likely to attend church. The choices people make during the early and middle years of adulthood have lasting consequences. By the time people reach middle age, their religious identities are largely set. Few people change religions after age fifty.

The period of adolescence and young adulthood is critical for forging the relationship between religion and politics. Political identities, such as being a Democrat or Republican, are shallow or absent in childhood. Children may parrot the beliefs of their parents, but they don't have a deep understanding of them. Then, just as adolescents are untethering themselves from their parents' religion, they become politically aware.

Political identity crystallizes during early adulthood, while young people are still at their furthest distance from religion. By the time they begin to form families and consider returning to the religious fold, most people have chosen sides in politics. It's not that they have formed detailed political ideologies—as chapter 3 discussed, most people never do. But they have aligned their sense of identity with social groups on one side or the other. We know who our people are by the time we reconsider who our gods are.

This middle phase of adulthood is when we sort ourselves into one denomination or another or away from religion entirely. People whose social identities are aligned with Republicans drift toward more fundamentalist denominations of Christianity. Those whose identities are aligned with Democrats, meanwhile, drift toward more progressive churches or away from religion.

Surveys suggest that the average American now perceives organized religion to be linked to Republicans more than Democrats. Christianity, in particular, has come to be seen as a Republican thing. So the same forces that attract young Republicans back into church are also pushing young Democrats away. The dramatic secularization of America in recent decades is driven mainly by Democrats and the social identities that are connected with that party. Since 2008, the rate of Republican "nones" has increased some, from 9 to 15 percent. But among Democrats, it jumped from 18 to 38 percent.

This perception that religion in general—and especially evangelical or born-again religious groups—is conservative is not an accident. Religious denominations have strategically positioned themselves to attract particular audiences and organize political alliances for centuries. The Southern Baptists, the largest evangelical Protestant group in the United States, split from the northern wing over slavery in 1845. It soon became the most prominent Christian church among southern enslavers. Throughout the Jim Crow era, the Southern Baptist Convention supported segregation. They apologized for these stances in 1995.

The modern-day "religious right" was forged as a response to the 1954 Supreme Court case *Brown v. Board of Education*, which declared racial segregation in schools to be unconstitutional. Desegregation efforts moved slowly, with lots of court-ordered injunctions and lawsuits delaying the process for years. During this time, private schools, typically Christian schools, proliferated. White children moved out of public schools into these segregated private schools, which came to be called "segregation academies."

More lawsuits challenged whether the *Brown* decision applied to these private schools or only to schools that receive taxpayer money. In 1969, a group of Black parents in Holmes County, Mississippi, filed a lawsuit arguing that segregated private schools should not be allowed tax-exempt status. As Black students in Holmes County began entering all-White public schools, White students fled. In 1971, the parents won their case, *Green v. Connally*, and the IRS withdrew tax-exempt status from racially segregated private schools. But by then, in many ways, it was too late. Between 1954 and 1971, White families had largely moved out of public schools. The families left in the public schools were mostly Black and Latino, and lower income. By 1970, there was not a single White student left in public school in Holmes County.

Historian Randall Balmer has documented how conservative activists in the 1970s, including Paul Weyrich, Pat Robertson, and Jerry Falwell, had been trying to build a voting coalition of evangelical Christian groups but were not getting much traction. They tried rallying evangelicals around school prayer and the threat of pornography, but those issues didn't work. They tried rallying around abortion. But in 1970, abortion was largely seen as a "Catholic issue" that few evangelical Protestants felt strongly about. In 1971 the Southern Baptist Convention even passed a resolution calling to legalize abortion. When *Roe v. Wade* was decided in 1973, evangelical Christians were split over it.

But when the IRS started enforcing tax requirements on segregated schools, the activists had found their rallying cry. The federal government, once again, was viewed as interfering in the business of (mostly) southern states. White and Black Protestant churches were already almost entirely segregated from each other. Before the *Brown* decision, public schools were racially segregated throughout the South. In the wake of that decision, segregation was maintained by White students moving to private religious schools. And now the IRS was threatening that arrangement as well.

The rallying cry worked. In the 1970s, only around 40 percent of White evangelicals identified as Republicans. By 2020, more than 70 percent were Republican and more than 80 percent voted for Donald Trump. Eventually, White evangelical leaders would form a consensus against abortion and against same-sex marriage. But it was debates over racial segregation that first began sorting Americans' racial and partisan identities together.

The sorting took some time to take effect. Ronald Reagan appealed to evangelicals in his rhetoric, but there was not a clear divide between evangelicals and others in the elections between 1980 and 1988. But once that sorting process started, it generated startling results. Once White Christians became almost synonymous with Republicans, young people who had drifted away from religion as teens and became Republicans in their twenties now joined Christian churches in their thirties. These trends were clear by 1992, when 86 percent of Republican presidential votes were cast by White Christians. This was a potent voting block, as White Christians made up 73 percent of the electorate.

At the same time, casting White Christians as Republicans pushed young Democrats in the opposite direction. Those who had become Democrats often didn't come back to religion at all. This political sorting has contributed to the decline of religion in America more generally. In a country that is about evenly divided between left and right, connecting Christianity to the right means that eventually the other half will not be Christian. We have already traveled well along this path. As I noted earlier in this chapter, nearly a third of American adults do not identify with any religion, and up to one fourth don't believe in God. What was once a huge voting block for Republicans is no more. In 2022, White Christians made up only half of the electorate, and their numbers are declining.

Learning about history and social trends can make you feel small. What you thought was your own private, unique experience so often turns out to be just an eddy in a stream much larger than yourself. We are swept along on these currents much more than we like to admit. A classic example is baby names, which offer an indirect indicator of cultural norms. Parents-to-be often give enormous amounts of thought to picking a name that feels right and that is distinctive enough but not too unusual. And yet, most parents end up choosing from among the same small set of newly popular names without realizing they are being influenced by social trends already under way. The parents of Jennifers in the 1970s and Olivias in the 2010s felt that they were striking out in new directions when they were really following trails.

Much the same thing is happening today, as we align our religious identities with our social-group identities in predictable ways. By the time I was in college, I was still grasping to understand liberal and conservative ideologies intellectually, but I felt my people were firmly on the progressive side. Just as Michele Margolis's research suggests, I had distanced myself from religion in my teens. I hadn't been to church since I graduated high school. I immersed myself in philosophy and theology classes in addition to my social science courses. I read Boethius and Thomas Aquinas, who strove to reconcile their Christian faith with reason. I read Bertrand Russell, who argued that there is no need for faith when there is evidence; that faith is what we call it when we substitute desires for reason.

At the same time, I was taking classes on logic and philosophy of science. I learned about truth tables, which allowed you to sort out the validity of complicated statements by simply adding up the truth values of their parts. They turned the crystalline clarity of algebra into the sledgehammer of logic. I learned about all the ways, deductive and inductive, to weigh up whether there was sufficient evidence to accept a conclusion. Most important, I learned that conclusions could be accepted only if there was good evidence for them.

And then, as my mind swirled back and forth between Aquinas and truth tables, I spent a semester reading Søren Kierkegaard. It was a kind of last straw for my religion. He believed that religious faith and reason were clearly in conflict. He was as disturbed as I had been since middle school with the paradoxes and contradictions of religion. In particular, the idea that an eternal, infinite God became incarnated as a temporal, finite human struck him as absurd. The idea that the infinite, ineffable God was also a personal God who concerned himself with human affairs was even more so. Faced with these insanities, Kierkegaard did the impossible: he embraced the absurd. He argued that if we rely on reason, we would never be able to believe in God, because it is all just too preposterous. So, he argued, the only thing to do is to believe anyway. To have faith, not just in the absence of evidence but knowing full well that one's faith is in contradiction to evidence and reason, was the point.

I couldn't believe that this philosopher, smart and otherwise apparently sane, was saying this. I kept my professor after class, trying to figure out if Kierkegaard was being serious, and if I was understanding him correctly. I suspected that maybe it was a satire or an elaborate parody. Maybe he was some Stephen Colbert–like character, tracing faith to its logical conclusions, contradictions, and absurdities, in order to mock the faithful. But no, my professor insisted, Kierkegaard meant exactly what he said.

"How are we supposed to take this seriously?" I asked her. I was treating my professor like the nuns, assuming that she believed in the texts that she was teaching and wanted us to believe as well. But she wasn't like the nuns. She said, "You don't have to take it seriously. You don't *have* to do anything. I just want you to understand it. What you do with it from there is up to you."

I realized then that I wanted to be a professor.

By the time I was in graduate school, my middle school doubts had become full-throated atheism. In my first year, Mom came to visit me in St. Louis. I thought it was my chance to impress her with how far I'd come. She thought it was her last chance to save my soul.

I gave her a campus tour. I led her up the grand steps of the main entrance, through the high arches of the red granite and white limestone buildings. We walked through the quad, green and quiet in the heat of summer. We stopped for coffee, and she was quiet. I asked what she thought of campus. "It's pretty," she said. Then after a moment, "You could feed a lot of people for what it cost to build that."

"You're right," I said, realizing how far apart our worlds had become.

As I drove her home, she used the three-hour drive to start a serious conversation. She asked me if I was ready to let Jesus back into my life. I gripped the steering wheel and looked at the road. "That's not what I'm focused on right now, Mom. . . ." But she was having none of that deflection. She asked if I had thought it through that if you believe in Jesus you can have eternal life when it turns out you were right. And if you were wrong then you lose nothing. On the other hand, if you refuse to believe, then you risk eternal damnation.

"Pascal's wager," I said.

"Who?"

"Never mind," I said. "The problem with that line of thinking is that there are not just two options to choose from. There are hundreds of gods to bet on. What if I choose Jesus but the Hindus turn out to be right? Or the Zoroastrians? What if I believe all the Christian stuff but I eat meat and the Jains are right? I'll never reach enlightenment."

"You can't think that way," she said. "Jesus said, 'I am the way, and the truth, and the life. No one comes to the Father, but through me.' It's in the Gospel."

"Why would I listen to Jesus about whether I should believe in Jesus?" I said. "Why would I believe in the Bible based on what it says in the Bible? That's circular reasoning. What if I wrote a book and the first page said, 'Everything in this book is true.' Is that good enough reason to believe everything else in that book?" We went on like that for miles, her treating the ride as a ministry, and me treating it as a graduate seminar, as we drove past the Native American burial mounds of southern Illinois. Ancient monuments to yet more gods, I thought, that I couldn't bring myself to bet on.

"You have to believe based on faith, not just reason," she said. "Human minds are too small to comprehend God." I heard the voice of Sister Mary as she said that.

"But if you believe without reason and evidence," I said, "then there's no way to know which things to believe and not to believe. If there's no reasoning, then there's no good reason to choose Jesus and not Allah."

"Allah! Why would you choose Allah?" she said, exasperation rising in her voice. "Jesus said, 'You did not choose me but I chose you!' We are God's people and he is our God."

"So it's a tribal thing then?"

We both stared forward as the flat fields of Illinois gave way to the rolling hills of Kentucky, the car quiet at last, but for the hum of the road.

EIGHT

UNBELIEVABLE

The truth is always an insult or a joke, lies are
generally tastier. We love them. The nature of lies is
to please. Truth has no concern for anyone's comfort.

—KATHERINE DUNN

There was a time in the 1860s when it was hard to find a sugar cube in the hotels and cafés of Washington, D.C. That was because John Smith Dye published a popular book in 1864 called *The Adder's Den: Or Secrets of the Great Conspiracy to Overthrow Liberty in America.* The book claimed that a sprawling conspiracy of southerners known as the Slave Power was secretly controlling the Union government through murder and extortion. The theory made sense to many northerners. In 1841, President William Henry Harrison had died just thirty-two days into his presidency. Dye explained this suspicious death as an assassination by arsenic poisoning because Harrison would not go along with a plan to annex Texas and expand slavery. He was succeeded by John Tyler, a defender of slavery. To northerners, what would seem more probable: a president who opposed the expansion of slavery happens to die just after taking office, only to be replaced by a proslavery president? Or that proslavery enemies in the South had something to do with it?

Then, in 1850, President Zachary Taylor died after just over a year in office. Although his views on slavery were murky, he did not advocate for the expansion of slavery. He was replaced by Millard Fillmore, who was seen as friendlier to the South. Another assassination by an untraceable poison, said Dye.

To top off this brazen aggression, in 1857, president-elect James Buchanan dined with leading politicians, both northern and southern, at the National Hotel in Washington. Dye claimed that agents of the Slave Power poisoned all the lump sugar in the hotel with arsenic in a diabolical attempt to wipe out the northern leaders but leave the southerners unscathed. Northerners, you see, drank tea with lump sugar, but southerners preferred coffee, sweetened with granulated sugar. Dye claimed that sixty northerners were poisoned and thirty-eight died.

There is no evidence that sixty politicians were poisoned at the National or that Harrison or Taylor were poisoned. But to the northern readers of *The Adder's Den*, those explanations felt plausible. If the Slave Power conspiracy seems far-fetched to us after a century and a half, it is not because it was particularly wild and implausible compared to other stories that many people believe today. After all, there really was an organized faction of proslavery southern enemies battling to preserve and expand slavery in the Civil War years. It was the Confederacy. What makes the theory unlikely to be true is that a coordinated band of southerners were able to pull the strings behind the scenes and successfully assassinate multiple leaders while leaving no evidence. If this conspiracy theory seems implausible to us today, it is simply because those enemies are not *our* enemies.

Today, we are awash in our own conspiracy theories and misinformation. Scrolling on Facebook just this morning, I saw people I know posting about how the IRS is sending armed agents to our doors, and how the Rothschilds control the world money supply. Interference with the Rothschild's schemes, the post said, caused the Second World War and, now, Russia's invasion of Ukraine. "Connecting the dots yet?" my high school friend wrote. He's not a rare exception. In 2020 and 2021, surveys indicated that a quarter of Americans believe the Rothschild family controls the world's governments and economies. A third of the population believes *someone* is secretly controlling world events other than officially recognized governments. Another quarter of Americans think it is George Soros, while a similar number think it is Charles Koch.

One of the most bizarre and pernicious conspiracy theories today is QAnon. The basic story is that Q, a government insider, has been sending adherents messages unveiling a vast conspiracy of sex-trafficking Democrats who make up a "deep state" that is secretly running the government. Donald Trump, however, has been secretly defending the country from this cabal. From there, the theory proliferates into a tangled thicket of different threads and subplots. Although only 6 percent of survey respondents in 2021 said they believed the QAnon theory when it was mentioned by name, many more endorsed parts of it. Thirty-four percent agreed that "elites, from government and Hollywood, are engaged in a massive child sex trafficking racket." And a stunning 44 percent endorsed the claim that "there is a 'deep state' embedded in the government that operates in secret and without oversight."

Although Q is new (it began in 2017), older conspiracy theories are still widespread. A fifth of Americans agree with each of the following: that Barack Obama faked his birth certificate, that government officials know cell phones cause cancer but won't do anything about it because corporations won't let them, and that the pharmaceutical and medical industries are conspiring to invent new diseases so they can profit from them. A third of the population thinks that humans have made contact with aliens, but the government is covering it up.

A mostly consensus view has emerged in academic and journalism circles about our present predicament. It says that we have a new epidemic of misinformation and conspiracy theories. The epidemic is primarily concentrated among Republicans. The epidemic is dangerous because it leads people to make bad choices and do irrational things on the basis of false information. But that consensus is not only psychologically unrealistic, it is also inconsistent with the most recent data on these trends. In this chapter I argue that every part of the consensus view is basically wrong, and I sketch a more realistic view grounded in how ordinary people think about truth and lies.

Why do so many people believe these implausible, often outrageous, ideas when there is no credible evidence? Some scholars argue that certain personality traits or cognitive styles explain some people's susceptibility. Others think the rise of social media is to blame. But I don't find either of those explanations particularly compelling. Something more fundamental about the way human minds work is going on here.

Consider the personality theory, which says that certain types of people are drawn to misinformation and conspiracy theories because of their personality traits. Most personality traits studied have not turned out to be related to conspiracy beliefs. The so-called Big Five traits (openness to experience, extroversion, conscientiousness, agreeableness, and neuroticism), for example, have correlations close to zero with conspiracy beliefs. One trait that does reliably correlate, however, is narcissism. Narcissists have an inflated sense of their own worth and tend toward grandiose notions of their own place in the world. They are self-centered and tend to become aggressive if their superiority is questioned. Some psychologists have argued that conspiracy theories fill the narcissists' need to feel that they know better than the official accounts. Conspiracy theories assure their adherents that what people see in the mainstream news is good enough for "normies," but only the select few have insight about the shadowy figures who are really in control.

The theory is plausible. And the correlation between narcissism and conspiracy beliefs is statistically significant. The only problem is that it's tiny. According to a review of all available studies, narcissism can explain about 7 percent of the variation in conspiracy beliefs. Most people are not narcissists. Scoring high on narcissism might nudge an individual a few percentage points toward believing a conspiracy theory, but it cannot begin to explain why huge segments of the population believe in them.

Another popular personality-based explanation is based on the "need for closure." People high in the need for closure want clear, concrete answers. They can't stand life's gray areas. So they tend to grab for any explanation that promises to provide a tidy resolution. Conspiracy theories, according to this view, offer a simple answer to life's complex questions. Again, the theory seems plausible, but the evidence is mixed.

Some conspiracy theories offer simpler answers than the mainstream account of things. For example, world events are so complex and confusing that it can be simpler to assume that someone like George Soros has it all under control. Even if you hate Soros, that conspiracy theory reassures you that the world is not complex and chaotic but orderly and supervised.

Other conspiracy theories are more mysterious and chaotic than the official evidence-based accounts. For example, the assassination of John F. Kennedy can be explained as the deranged act of Lee Harvey Oswald. It is difficult for many people to believe that a great man like Kennedy could be brought down by a random guy with a rifle, so they instead believe that a vast conspiracy involving Russians and the Mafia was behind it (56 percent of Americans believe this conspiracy theory). That explanation seems weightier, somehow, because in that version of events it took a powerful and coordinated enemy to bring down a great leader. But the explanation only raises more questions. How did they pull it off? Who exactly was in charge? And what were the motives of the various parties? Conspiracy theorists have answers for all these questions, of course, but their justifications are not the kind of crisp, neat resolution that satisfies a person's need for closure.

One study found that higher need for closure was associated with greater belief in conspiracy theories that provide clear answers. But it was also correlated with *less* belief in conspiracy theories that did not provide clear answers. In other words, there was nothing special about the closure-inducing power of conspiracy theories. People high in need for closure, by definition, want closure. If a conspiracy theory can provide it, then fine. But if not, then they will search for closure elsewhere. There does not seem to be a strong connection between closure and conspiracies in general.

Probably the best-studied individual difference is a kind of cognitive style: intuitive versus analytic thinking. People who are intuitive thinkers go with their gut response. Those who are analytic thinkers reflect carefully and treat everything like a logic problem. An example of a question used to measure this factor is: "Emily's father has three daughters. The first two are named April and May. What is the third daughter's name?" The intuitive answer is June, but a moment's reflection reveals that it must be Emily. Research suggests that intuitive thinkers are a bit more likely to endorse conspiracy theories than analytic thinkers are. But again, the differences are small, explaining less than 5 percent of the variation in conspiracy beliefs. Explanations based on personality traits and thinking styles have a grain of truth, but they leave the lion's share of the phenomenon unexplained.

What about social media? These platforms are increasingly the way that misinformation spreads because of the ways their algorithms interact with human psychology. Algorithms are simply bits of computer code that measure what kinds of posts are getting the most likes, clicks, and shares, and move more of that kind of content to the top of people's feeds. The details of how the algorithms work at companies like Facebook, X, YouTube, Instagram, and TikTok are closely guarded secrets. But they all perform essentially the same function. Engineers don't preprogram them to favor some types of information over others. The algorithms learn that from human users.

What makes human users engage with a post is emotion. Any emotion is better than no emotion, but moral emotions, like shame, awe, and contempt, are especially powerful. And for making a post go viral, moral outrage is the most powerful accelerant of all. When deciding whether to share political content, people prefer to share true over false information, but they don't have direct access to the truth. As we saw in chapter 2, they use partisan-based motivated reasoning to judge what is true.

And so, the standard story goes, we share a biased set of information, and the algorithms magnify that bias. Add that to the fact that people create like-minded social networks by following people who are already on the same team, and you have the often-bemoaned problem of echo chambers. Social media makes it easy to never see the perspective of the other side, except when mocking it.

It is undeniable that social media facilitates the spread of misinformation. And yet, there is reason to doubt whether social media is really a fundamental cause of it. If social media really was a major cause of why so many people believe lies, then we would expect to see the prevalence of misinformation beliefs rise along with the popularity of social media. But we haven't. A massive study led by political scientist Joseph Uscinski examined the proportion of Americans and residents of six European countries who believed dozens of different conspiracy theories, spanning the past fifty years. Astonishingly, belief in conspiracy theories is generally no higher today than it was in the 1970s.

To be sure, people believe a lot of weird things today. But we tend to forget that people have always believed a lot of weird things. In 1981, 48 percent of Americans believed that Robert Kennedy's assassination was a conspiracy rather than the act of a lone gunman. In 2021, 43 percent believed that. In 1966, 50 percent believed John F. Kennedy's assassination was a conspiracy, and in 2021, 56 percent agreed. In 1996, 49 percent of Americans believed that humans had made contact with aliens, but the government was covering up evidence of UFOs. In 2021, that figure was 50 percent.

The particular conspiracy theories that are popular, of course, change with time. There were no QAnon or COVID conspiracy theories in the 1990s, for example. But in 1995, a third of Americans believed that police conspired to frame O. J. Simson for murder. In 2021 only 11 percent believed that. In 1991, 40 percent of Americans believed that Ronald Reagan conspired with the Iranian government to hold American hostages until after the 1980 election. Only 12 percent believed that in 2021. Part of the reason these conspiracies have fallen out of favor is that many young adults have never heard of O. J. Simpson or the Iranian hostage crisis. Uscinski's study found that some conspiracy theories became more popular over time, while others faded away. But the proportion of the population endorsing conspiracy theories overall has been more or less constant for fifty years.

That stability contradicts the idea that the rise of social media has fueled an epidemic of misinformation and conspiracy theories. In fact, in contrast to nearly everyone's strong intuition, there does not seem to be an epidemic. Or at least, not more of an epidemic than there was in the 1980s, 1990s, and early 2000s. People today believe a lot of false information. But, despite all the talk of a new "post-truth world," the evidence suggests that humans have never been particularly attached to truth. The biggest effect of social media may ironically be that we are simply more aware of how many false things other people believe.

From the evidence reviewed so far, there seems to be very little that is unique about misinformation and conspiracy theories. People treat them much like other kinds of identity-relevant information, as tools they pick up and lay down as needed to defend their psychological bottom lines. How, then, do we explain the apparently massive partisan asymmetries in conspiracy beliefs? Why, for example, is there no left-wing counterpart to QAnon or the Big Lie about the 2020 election being stolen? Surely, one might think, this is one area where the minds of conservatives and the minds of liberals are truly different.

Not so fast. Recent research suggests Republicans are more likely to believe in *certain kinds* of conspiracy theories. About half of Republicans believe that President Obama was not really born in the United States. Republicans are also much more likely to believe that COVID risk was overstated, that Biden stole the 2020 election, that climate change is a hoax, and that George Soros secretly runs the world.

At the same time, Democrats are much more likely to believe in other kinds of conspiracy theories. About 70 percent of Democrats believe that Russian operatives have been secretly manipulating American national policy. Democrats are also much more likely to believe that Republicans stole the 2000, 2004, and 2016 elections, that Trump covered up the severity of his COVID symptoms, and also that Trump faked having COVID at all.

The critical ingredient, argues the study's author Adam Enders, is who the villain is. His study, the most comprehensive to date, tested fifty-two conspiracy theories among Americans and another twenty conspiracy theories in six countries around the world and found no general difference in levels of conspiracy beliefs between right-wing and left-wing voters. People on the left and right simply believed different conspiracy theories.

When this paper was published, a lot of readers were skeptical. The prevailing consensus among academics, who tend to lean left, was that conspiracy thinking is especially common on the right. Some questioned whether the particular conspiracy theories tested were cherry-picked. Maybe the authors—intentionally or unintentionally—selected a biased set of conspiracy theories that would overestimate support among Democrats to make them look similar to Republicans. But the authors had anticipated this objection.

In a follow-up study, they ran a clever experiment to rule out this kind of cherry-picking. They made up five new conspiracy theories and asked respondents whether they believed them. For each conspiracy they made two versions: one in which Republicans were the villains and one in which Democrats were the villains. For example: "Do you think that Republican political elites are secretly plotting with large banks to lie about the health of the economy to gain support for their economic policy proposals?" Or, "Do you think that Democratic political elites are secretly working with political extremists to undermine the American government for their own gain?"

When Republicans were the bad guys, Democrats tended to believe the theory, and when Democrats were the villains, Republicans believed. The effects of simple partisanship were much larger than any of the other factors, like personality traits or cognitive style, that researchers have investigated. It turns out that if you make up just about any lie about the out-group, many people will believe it. And even if they don't believe it, partisans do not think badly of the liar, as long as they are lying about the other side.

There is a difference between the parties when it comes to misinformation, but it is not in the minds of the voters. It is found in the behavior of political elites. Donald Trump's biggest insight was to realize that there is literally no limit to the lies, scandals, and crimes that partisans will accept as long as they are done in service of *us* against *them* identity fights. But in Democratic circles there is a strong assumption that liberal voters are too smart, too educated, or too rational to fall for such lies. The data suggests otherwise. If the research is correct, it is only a matter of time before liberal politicians and media elites start testing the limits of mendacity. I expect they will find that people are willing to accept an outrageous level of dishonesty, as long as it is in service of their social identities.

One reason that so many people wring their hands about the spread of misinformation is that we worry that the more plentiful it is, the more people will be misled. And the more people are misled, the more they will make bad decisions. This is what economists might call a "supply-side theory." It says that when lies are plentiful, people will consume more of them. This view treats people as dupes, cluelessly accepting the narratives that politicians and propagandists dole out to them. But as we saw in chapter 2, people are active curators of their own beliefs, filtering and revising to keep their beliefs in support of their psychological bottom line. People have a demand, in other words, for certain kinds of lies.

On Monday, October 4, 2021, an engineer at Facebook made an error in a line of code that completely disconnected the company from the internet. From 10:40 a.m. to 5:30 p.m. central time, the world's most popular social media platform was offline. According to the supply-side view that social media drives most misinformation, that outage would provide a blessed day of drastically reduced misinformation. But if people demand to be lied to, then they could find the misinformation they want elsewhere. And that is just what they did. A study led by political scientist Matt Motta found that during the hours of the outage, Google searches surged for misinformation-heavy sites like Infowars and keywords for specific false stories such as Ivermectin and microchips. This natural experiment suggests that people are not passive dupes, but rather they seek out the stories they want to be told. If one channel shuts down, they just find another.

This give-and-take between the supply of misinformation and the demand for it creates what philosopher Daniel Williams calls a "rationalization market." He argues that there is a literal marketplace, not just of ideas but of rationalizations. He starts with the premise that people work hard to adopt beliefs that make them feel happy and fit in well with the groups they care about. In the language of chapter 2, people deploy their psychological immune systems in service of their psychological bottom line that they are good and reasonable people and their groups are too.

Williams notes, also consistent with chapter 2, that we can't simply decide to believe just any ludicrous thing we want to believe, because we would look foolish to ourselves and others. Instead, we have to find plausible-seeming reasons that allow us to believe the things we want while seeming reasonable. That need creates a demand for rationalizations.

Where there is a demand, some ambitious entrepreneur will spring up to fill it. Politicians and pundits (as well as marketers, preachers, influencers, and so on) will provide the rationalizations that people want in return for attention, status, power, and profit. Different groups want different rationalizations, so the suppliers will tend to specialize into parties, channels, and websites that cater to different groups. Some rationalization vendors will be better than others, and the ones that outperform their competitors will grow rich and influential.

The storylines they provide are not necessarily false. In fact, it is often easier and more persuasive to create rationalizations using mostly true information, selectively spun, rather than blatant lies. But since the point of a rationalization is to sound reasonable rather than be true, either true or false stories will do. The purpose is to allow us to do what we want to do and to feel how we want to feel, while being considered good, reasonable members of our groups. Rationalization vendors provide us with talking points that we can use in arguments with other people or—just as important—in our own inner dialogues.

Thinking about misinformation through the lens of rationalization markets clarifies so much. For one thing, it helps us understand why despite social media enabling the rapid spread of lies and conspiracy theories, the average person is not any more misinformed than they were fifty years ago. Supermarkets today have dozens of brands of toothpaste, far more than they had in 1970. That allows people more choice in the particular brands and flavors, but they don't necessarily buy more toothpaste, because the demand for it has not changed. Social media is like a giant supermarket of information, both true and false. People can find whatever niche rumor or conspiracy theory they need to rationalize the choices they want to make. But having a bigger supermarket doesn't increase the appetite for rationalizations overall.

Understanding rationalization markets puts the threat of misinformation in its proper context. The main reason people hate misinformation is that we fear it will mislead people into making bad decisions. (Research suggests that we are not worried about being misled ourselves. It is only other people who we worry are vulnerable to being duped.) If people believe that COVID vaccines are government plots to implant microchips in citizens, then we fear they won't get vaccinated. If people believe that Democrats are Satan-worshipping pedophiles, then we fear they will vote for someone like Donald Trump. This fear implies that if we could only correct that misinformation, then we could change their behavior.

It doesn't work that way. Consider a study led by political

scientist Brendan Nyhan that surveyed voters just after Donald Trump's convention speech during the 2016 race. The speech contained a lot of lies, such as the claim that violent-crime rates were rising dramatically when, in fact, they had fallen dramatically. Nyhan and colleagues measured how much voters believed several such pieces of misinformation, before and after providing fact-checks to correct misperceptions.

In an initial survey, Trump supporters believed the claim of rising crime more than Clinton supporters did. Then the researchers provided respondents with a fact-check that read, "According to FBI's Bureau of Justice Statistics, the violent crime rate has fallen dramatically and consistently over time. According to their estimates, the homicide rate in the U.S. in 2015 was half that recorded in 1991." The fact-check worked. Both Trump and Clinton supporters reported substantially lower perceptions of crime immediately following the correction (although Trump supporters still thought crime was higher than Clinton supporters). After several such fact-checks, participants were reporting beliefs that were much more in line with reality.

Mission accomplished, right? Well, yes and no. If the goal is simply to make people's beliefs more accurate, then the fact-checks worked. But when the researchers measured participants' support for Trump and Clinton and who they planned to vote for, the fact-checks had no impact. That's because the vast majority of the information people talk about as reasons to support one politician or another are not really the causes of their decisions. They are rationalizations. People supported Trump or Clinton because of their social-group identities. They picked up true or false beliefs as needed to provide reasons for what they wanted to do anyway.

This same dynamic happens with political advertising. The

vast majority of the funds raised by campaigns are spent on political ads. The assumption is that the ads let them get their message out to constituents and hopefully persuade some undecided voters. Spending in the 2024 presidential election is expected to be more than $12 billion, and new records are set every election cycle. Some ads are truthful, some are misleading, and pundits worry a lot about whether dishonest advertising will lead unsuspecting voters to make bad choices.

They probably shouldn't worry so much. Despite all the money, political advertising has almost no effect. The largest study done to date examined the causal impact of forty-nine different political ads run during the 2016 presidential race. The average effect was to shift vote choices by only seven tenths of 1 percent (not statistically significant from zero). Advertising effects were tiny or absent for Republicans, Democrats, and Independents alike.

So why do political campaigns spend so much money if advertising has almost no effect? Because from the politician's point of view, getting even a few hundred or a few thousand extra votes might mean the difference between winning or losing a close race. All the money and the constant barrage of ads around election time creates a false impression of advertising's importance—it seems like ads must be important because they are everywhere. But like other kinds of information and misinformation, political ads are just the supply side. People have to have a demand for that information in order to use it. As a result, every ad preaches to the choir. In 99.3 percent of cases, we use political messaging as a rationalization for how we already plan to vote.

In a way, we are fortunate that people do not act on all their political beliefs. When Edgar Maddison Welch got up before dawn, loaded his assault rifle in his car, and drove from Salisbury, North

Carolina, to Washington, D.C., he was being logically consistent. He believed the conspiracy theory that a ring of Satan-worshipping Democrats were sexually abusing children in the basement of Comet Ping Pong, a D.C. pizzeria. No one seemed to be doing anything about it, so he would.

He knew the mission would be dangerous. He described his plan to a friend he hoped would join him as "Raiding a pedo ring, possibly sacraficing [sic] the lives of a few for the lives of many," he wrote. "Standing up against a corrupt system that kidnaps, tortures and rapes babies and children in our own backyard." Welch realized he might not come back. On the drive, he recorded a video of himself speaking to his two young daughters. "I can't let you grow up in a world that's so corrupt by evil, without at least standing up for you and for other children just like you."

When Welch walked into the pizza place with his AR-15 in his hands and a Colt revolver on his hip, customers started scrambling for the exits. Welch searched for the basement dungeon, but there was no basement. He found a locked door, and he shot the lock. But it was just a computer closet. Eventually, he put down his guns and walked out, hands raised, to be arrested by the many police who were by now on the scene.

It is easy to shake our heads at Welch's seemingly absurd actions. And yet, there were millions of people within a day's drive of Washington, D.C., who believed the PizzaGate conspiracy at the time. That conspiracy soon grew into QAnon, which millions more endorse today. If you believed children were being abused nearby, wouldn't you want to do something about it? Wouldn't most people? The really striking thing is that many more believers have not carried out similar missions.

Mr. Welch is remarkable, not because he believed a bizarre

conspiracy theory like millions of other people, but because he used that belief as a cause of his actions and not just a rationalization. For the vast majority of believers in PizzaGate and QAnon, the main point is that they hate Democrats and love Republicans. The Satan-worshipping and pedophilia seem like plausible enough stories to accept about people you find morally repugnant for other reasons. But belief in those claims is incredibly shallow, in the sense that it rarely leads to actions. For most people, they are merely rationalizations to back up why their team is good and the other team is bad.

Some analysts have tried to distinguish people's true beliefs from "expressive responding." The idea is that people often endorse falsehoods on surveys not because they really believe them, but because they want to express solidarity with their identity-based groups. In some cases that surely happens, but it is unlikely to explain most cases where people profess a belief that is false. The distinction between true beliefs and expressive responding assumes that there is a crisp line in people's minds between true and false ideas in the first place. We get this idea from mundane, concrete beliefs people might have in everyday life. If I believe my keys are in the drawer, I know they are not in the car. I might be mistaken, but I have a clear idea in my mind about what is true.

Compare that to the vague statements and fuzzy ideas that make up most political discourse. Do Democrats want to destroy the country? Is Trump's philosophy "semi-fascist," as Joe Biden remarked in a controversial speech? Does one group stand for the "real America"? These claims are so murky that they could mean any number of things.

Even concrete facts like the size of Donald Trump's inauguration crowd or the number of people killed by guns each day in the United States are often interpreted loosely. People understand factual statements as being about a broader "gist meaning" and don't get too hung up on the details. To a Trump supporter, when Trump and his administration lied about the size of his inauguration crowd, the gist meaning was that a lot of Americans support him. When Biden supporters were asked whether it was true that five hundred Americans are killed by guns each day, it sounded true to many, even though the actual number is a fourth that number. The gist idea they were endorsing is that gun violence is far too common.

On a recent road trip, my brother-in-law admired a Maserati that zoomed past us. "How much do you think that costs?" he asked. Another relative said, "Joe Biden wants to cap them at fifty thousand dollars." I invited him to take out his phone and look up any evidence for that claim. Knowing he was caught spinning a rationalization, he revised and changed tacks. "That's just an example," he said, his voice angry. "It's not about Maseratis. The point is that that's the kind of socialist thing Biden wants to do." Everyone stopped talking about it. We had a long ride ahead of us.

When confronted about a lie or fact-checked on misinformation, people have a few options to resolve their cognitive dissonance while preserving their psychological bottom line. Sometimes they double down and defend the lie. One easy route is to denigrate the source of the fact-checking by claiming, for example, that the mainstream media is biased. But if the lie is easily debunked, a better strategy is a tactical retreat to the broader gist meaning. Sometimes the gist is simply "the other team is bad," which can justify believing nearly anything. Often it does, at least for the moment.

Fact-checking claims that are used as identity-based rationalizations is more likely to anger someone than correcting ordinary false beliefs. If I think my keys are in the drawer but you point out that I left them in the car, I don't get mad—you have helped me. But the function of identity-based rationalizations is to assert that I am a good and reasonable person. If you correct my rationalization, then you are challenging the idea that I am a good and reasonable person. So people dig in, counterargue, and refuse to concede the argument. This creates the impression that the belief must be especially important and powerful.

And yet, studies that have tracked misinformation and conspiracy theory beliefs over time have found that they are incredibly flimsy. People flip-flop all the time. In chapter 3 we saw that the vast majority of people have little coherence or stability in their beliefs about political issues. It turns out that conspiracy beliefs are no more logically coherent or stable over time than other ordinary issue beliefs. Even when people express total certainty, their answers are only slightly more consistent over time than if they were randomly choosing answers from a hat. The conspiracy theory that your uncle insists on today might be forgotten about next month, replaced with some other identity-based rationalization. Ironically, beliefs that are most closely tied to our identities are the most likely to be rationalizations that follow from what we want to do rather than actually drive our actions.

Should we even bother trying to correct misinformation, then? Should social media platforms tag falsehoods as false? Should we challenge our friends and relatives who repeat those lies and conspiracy theories? I believe we should, but we should expect the process to be frustrating and often unsuccessful. Studies suggest that the impact of most kinds of corrections will be small and short-lived and are not likely to change people's behavior in the vast majority of cases.

Still, if even a few people are dissuaded from taking an assault rifle into a pizzeria or are encouraged to vaccinate themselves against a dangerous disease, it is worth the effort. One of the most effective ways to combat misinformation is known as "inoculation." Just as a vaccine prepares a person's immune system to defend against a later infection, information inoculation primes people's psychological immune system to defend against false information. For example, a social media campaign might warn users that highly emotional words like *terrifying* or *disgusting* are often used to capture people's attention and increase the viral spread of false information.

In interpersonal situations, it is often too late to warn people about misinformation ahead of time. We usually only react when we hear someone repeat false information that they have already accepted. In such cases, our gut response is simply to contradict the false information, but that is a mistake. It quickly turns into a back-and-forth argument. And the more you talk about false information, the more likely people are to remember that false information as if it were true. A better technique is what some researchers call a "truth sandwich." Rather than starting by refuting the false information, you start by stating the truth as plainly as possible. Then acknowledge the misinformation and explain why it is incorrect. Then—and this is critical—end by repeating or rephrasing the fact again. Stating the truth at the beginning and the end helps make it clear and easy to remember.

Techniques like inoculation and truth sandwiches have been shown in studies to be more effective at changing beliefs than the typical ways we argue with each other. And yet, it is a mistake to expect that we will change someone's politics by changing any particular belief. As we have seen, belief in misinformation and conspiracy theories is usually a rationalization aimed at defending something deeper: social identity. As we will see in the final chapter, connecting to others at that deeper level sometimes means giving up the goal of changing them at all.

NINE

WINGING IT TOGETHER

The Earth is a very small stage in a vast cosmic arena. Think of the endless cruelties visited by the inhabitants of one corner of this pixel on the scarcely distinguishable inhabitants of some other corner, how frequent their misunderstandings, how eager they are to kill one another, how fervent their hatreds. Think of the rivers of blood spilled by all those generals and emperors so that, in glory and triumph, they could become the momentary masters of a fraction of a dot.

—CARL SAGAN

There is a magnolia tree in my yard that has seen me through some hard times. After Donald Trump won the presidency in 2016, I spent a lot of time under that tree. I stopped reading the news and tried to stop thinking about politics. I kept telling myself that the sun would still rise every morning. It would burn off the dew from those waxy green leaves like it did before. I watched a beetle crawling on the rosebushes beneath the magnolia, and I imagined it was me, happily oblivious to what happened outside my little circle of care.

When the world is difficult, it is tempting to withdraw. Whether it is to the tangible comforts of a garden or the soothing self-righteousness of our favorite political echo chambers, we often prefer escape to dealing with the problems in front of us. That's understandable. It's human. But it's not enough. Because eventually we have to look up from our backyards and our social media platforms and remember that the world is still there, and we still belong in it. We have to find a way to live together.

So let's take stock of where we are today. We are evenly divided between right and left. Not based on ideologies, which few ordinary people have. We are divided by our social identities and by the stories we spin to reassure ourselves that we and our groups are good, reasonable people.

Those who are born White tend to see today's unequal power structures as legitimate, based on differences between groups' abilities or work ethic. If they are born in a place where ancient chalk made cotton and slavery profitable, and hence has greater racial inequality today, they are even more likely to see things that way. The less formal education they have, the easier it is to believe that narrative. Once that worldview is in place, people tend to drift toward more conservative forms of Christianity and rural places, where others like them tend to share their views.

Those who are born into non-White families tend to see today's inequalities as unfair products of past and present discrimination. That is even more likely if they are born in places where cotton and slavery were profitable. Some White Americans share this view, but it is more likely among those with more formal education. These left-leaning identities and educational experiences attract people to big cities and away from organized religion. They end up in diverse, educated social circles that reaffirm their group identities.

We all feel that we have reasoned our way to our own core

principles. And in a sense, we have. We have thought through lots of issues and settled on answers that make sense from where we are standing. The trouble is that these identity-based paths of thought are leading us into ever more heated conflict with one another and carrying us away from friends and family. Surveys suggest that between 20 to 25 percent of Americans are now estranged from a loved one because of politics. The percentage of people who report strongly disliking the opposing party has increased by 400 percent in the last twenty years. Most of this book has been focused on explaining why our social identities line up so closely with our political identities, but those have been gradual changes over many decades. What explains the spike in partisan animosity over the last two decades? The basic psychology of partisanship has not changed. It is the environment that changed.

The demographic groups that underpin our social identities have been undergoing gradual changes that, together, are suddenly no longer gradual. Since 1980, the share of White Americans declined from 80 percent of the population to 60 percent. During that time, the Hispanic population has grown from 7 percent to 19 percent, while the share of the population that is Black has remained steady at around 12 to 13 percent.

The religious composition of America is also changing. Christians made up about 90 percent of the population in 1980, but only 64 percent today. Meanwhile the nonreligious grew from 5 percent to 30 percent. As I've mentioned, the Brookings Institution predicts that the nonreligious will outnumber Christians sometime around 2070. The population is also becoming more educated. In 1980, only one in five Americans had a college degree. But today, nearly 40 percent do. And 14 percent have a graduate or professional degree.

These trends, on their own, have been gradual rather than dramatic changes. But the groups that make up the core of the Republican Party are all declining, while the groups that lean Democrat are all expanding. Since 1976, White Christians declined from 80 percent of the population to just 44 percent today. As recently as 2006, White evangelical Christians made up 23 percent of the population, but today they are only 15 percent. And the share without a college degree is smaller still. The American population is growing more diverse, better educated, more urban, and less religious.

We are at a precarious moment in history, where two trends are crossing each other. The first is that the Republican Party became a uniformly conservative party and the Democratic Party became consistently liberal. The second is that demographic changes, and the social identities that accompany them, are making for fewer and fewer Republicans. Right now we are on a knife's edge, where the electorate's power is evenly divided. In a country with two hundred million adults, a few thousand votes in a handful of states is enough to swing national elections. Once demographic change produces a decisive change in social identities, it is likely to be forever. So every election feels like a desperate last chance.

Some look at these trends and see an easy path to victory for Democrats. But that's not likely to happen anytime soon. Democrats already outnumber Republicans, and they have won the popular vote in seven out of the last eight presidential elections. But presidents aren't elected by the popular vote, and the electoral college favors the small rural states that lean Republican. The Senate also favors small, rural states, giving as much power to Wyoming as to New York.

On top of these structural Republican advantages, state legislatures are gerrymandering more extremely and more effectively than ever before, which further insulates politicians from the voters. The fact that Democrats are clustered together in cities makes it easy to pack them into a few gerrymandered districts, handing many more districts to rural Republican areas. Donald Trump's denial of his loss to Joe Biden has made election denial an acceptable strategy for Republicans who lose elections; false claims of voter fraud have been invoked by many Republican candidates since. And voter suppression laws that selectively discourage voting among poor, Black, and Hispanic voters are being passed at an accelerating pace in Republican-controlled states. Nineteen restrictive new laws passed in 2021 alone.

As the pressure of demographic change mounts, it forces Republicans to choose between maintaining power and maintaining a democracy. Anyone who thinks that people of good conscience will stand up and check the worst impulses of the politicians has not properly understood the psychological immune system. The vast majority of Republicans will easily rationalize such steps as necessary for the greater good of the country. If that outrages you, remember that Democrats would likely do the same if their positions were reversed. Rationalization is bipartisan.

The forces of demographic change are powerful. And so are antidemocratic reactions against it. Anyone who says they know how this conflict will turn out isn't telling the truth. But regardless of which side gains power at any given time, we can predict how the conflict will be perceived by both sides and the kinds of rationalizations they are likely to use to keep their psychological bottom lines intact. It is time to stop falling for the idea that surely *this* will be the last straw—the political outrage that changes people's minds. Instead, it is time to look plainly at why people believe what they believe, choose what they choose, and want what they want.

We need to look past people's reasons and think about the causes of their reasons. In this chapter, I will offer a series of questions to ask yourself to help reorient your thinking about political disagreements by focusing on how people are trying to defend their psychological bottom line. Answering those questions requires thinking about your own ideas—and those of the people who disagree with you—from the outside. It can be hard to do, especially for issues that we care deeply about. But thinking about disagreements this way offers the possibility of viewing divisive issues with calm, clarity, and compassion. It may even help to make changes in the world.

To many Republicans, the changing American population feels like a tragedy. The groups (mostly White, mostly Christian) who have dominated American politics and culture for the past two centuries are becoming a minority. That simple demographic fact feels to many like "real Americans" are being replaced by illegitimate outsiders. It is little wonder the replacement conspiracy theory—that Democrats are intentionally flooding the country with illegal immigrants to replace White Americans—has taken hold so easily.

To Democrats, changing demographics feels like long-overdue progress. We now have the prospect of a young, diverse, multicultural America committed to tearing down old power structures. It seems like the natural extension, not only of the civil rights movement but of the Enlightenment itself. Efforts by Republicans to resist those changes are seen as simple racism.

From the vantage point of history, America is changing fast. But from the perspective of a human life, these changes are grindingly slow. For at least the last few hundred years, it is the fate of conservatives to always be losing, but not quite yet. And it is the fate of progressives to always be winning, but not fast enough. The result is that progressives are winning, but only conservatives can see it. So everyone is miserable.

Everyone wants to know how we can bridge divides and get along better, as if we are going to return to a time when we all got along. But that time never really existed. America has been fraught with political conflict since its inception. The times when it seemed most peaceful and harmonious were the times when the majority so completely dominated the minority that no dissent could be heard. There is a lot of nostalgia for the 1950s, when Republicans and Democrats were not constantly at each other's throats. But that was because the southern wing of the Democratic Party so completely disenfranchised Black citizens that they had virtually no voice in American political life. It was a false peace, arranged between White Democrats and White Republicans, built on domination. As the civil rights era progressed, the prospect of a truly multiracial democracy came along with increased conflict and animosity. What we face today is the possibility that a multiracial coalition may for the first time have more political power than White Christians. The great question of our time is whether our Republic can survive that and remain a democracy.

At the level of national politics, I am not sure there is any clear way to break the fever of partisan hostility anytime soon. We can strengthen democracy with policies. Ending partisan gerrymandering, restoring the Voting Rights Act, and banning voting suppression tactics, for example, would make us a truer democracy. But they would only increase the rancor among those who view the majorities empowered by those policies as illegitimate holders of power.

This is a frustrating, heartbreaking position to be in. And yet, so many of us still want to somehow overcome political divides to stay connected with our friends and family. Every letter to an advice column seems to express this longing. Dear therapist: I can't stand my brother-in-law. Dear therapist: my sister constantly complains but won't do anything to change things. Dear therapist: my husband can't stop drinking. Dear therapist: my dad has been sucked down a black hole of conspiracy theories.

One response to all these problems is to just leave. And yet, it is not as if the letter writers have not thought of that. They have thought of that a thousand times before they write a letter, or go to therapy, or read a book about estrangement. The reason they have not walked away is that they want more. They want the other person integrated into their lives one way or another. That refusal to walk away is itself a kind of hope.

The next time you are tempted to get into a political argument rather than walk away, pause and ask yourself: Why do I want to engage here? When we are arguing with strangers on the internet, the motivation is too often that we want to argue them into submission or publicly embarrass them. But when it is a loved one, the motivation is often to restore a connection that is lost or strained. Plainly admitting our motivation to ourself can prevent a lot of useless conflict, especially with individuals we know and care about. If you look inside and find that your motivation is to prove them wrong or win the argument, you have already lost. If you want to find ways to understand and connect, there are ways to do that. Psychologists know a few things about how to bridge divides at the one-on-one level.

HIDDEN COMMON GROUND

One powerful strategy for rekindling connections focuses on the fact that we routinely exaggerate the differences between our own side and the other side. Psychologist Jake Westfall analyzed many years of survey and polling data to look at how Republicans and Democrats responded to a variety of political topics. Republicans, for example, were more likely to say that the government should reduce spending on providing services to the poor, whereas Democrats tended to say the government should increase spending. Republicans, on average, said that Black Americans should do more to help themselves, while Democrats said that the government should do more to help Black Americans. Republicans tended to say we should increase defense spending, but Democrats said we should reduce it. The list goes on, and the differences are basically in the directions you would expect.

But here's the important part: the differences between Republicans and Democrats were tiny. On a 6-point scale from "strongly agree" to "strongly disagree," the average differences were only about 1 point. When Westfall asked survey respondents to guess the response of the average Republican and Democrat, their assumptions were wildly exaggerated, often more than double the real level of disagreement. The more partisan the respondent was, the more they exaggerated the differences. And the more they exaggerated the differences, the more partisans disliked one another. As political scientist Lilliana Mason has argued, the average Democrat and Republican actually agree on far more than they disagree, when it comes to policies. And yet, they feel like they are further away than ever. In Mason's memorable phrase, we are in a state of uncivil agreement.

These studies of exaggerations in policy attitudes are important, but I don't think they go to the heart of the issue. As we saw in chapter 3, most people do not have clearly defined policy attitudes to begin with. On the one hand, this can be viewed as evidence that we agree on more than we think we do. But I suspect it usually means that issues and policies are not really what our deepest conflicts are about. When asked if they agree or disagree with specific policies, most people shrug and indicate an answer somewhere in the middle.

A related set of studies gets closer to the heart of the matter. We don't only exaggerate how much the other side disagrees with us. We also exaggerate how much the other side hates us. Psychologist Samantha Moore-Berg and colleagues found that, as in previous research, Republicans and Democrats tended to dislike each other and to rate each other as less fully human compared to how they rated members of their own party. But when asked to guess how each group responded, partisans on both sides greatly exaggerated how much the other side disliked and dehumanized their own side.

We are a divided country, but we are even more divided in our minds than in reality. Seeing each other as we really are is a simple—but not always easy—way to reduce the temperature. To bring that hidden common ground to light, we must slow down and actually ask, rather than assume, what the other person believes. So the next time you find yourself in a disagreement, ask your opponent: What exactly do you think here? And ask yourself: How far apart are we really?

INDIVIDUALS NOT GROUPS

Joseph Stalin and Mother Teresa didn't agree on much. But they both had the same insight about how differently we treat people as individuals compared to how we treat them in groups. Mother Teresa was concerned about how viewing people as nameless, faceless crowds makes us less likely to help the poor. "If I look at the mass, I will never act," she said. "If I look at the one, I will." Stalin's concern was different. He is reputed to have said, "The death of one man is a tragedy. The death of a million is a statistic." What both of them noticed is that we feel more empathy for the plight of an individual than for many individuals at once. Logically, this makes little sense. If one person's life is precious, then a thousand lives are a thousand times as precious. And yet, Stalin's and Teresa's insight has been supported again and again in research studies and in daily life. People feel more compassion, donate more money, and are more likely to go out of their way to help a single individual compared to a group of people.

We see an individual as more human than a group. In research led by psychologist Erin Cooley, we found that people could easily switch between viewing a collection of people as individuals versus as a group. For example, research participants attributed more humanity and felt more compassion for a set of ten individual refugees compared to when the same refugees were described as "a group of refugees." Our ability to toggle between viewing others as individuals versus groups is important because it means that we have the ability to dial our compassion up or down at will.

When it comes to partisan politics, it is easy to see the other side as a faceless mob intent on doing harm. But when we think of an opponent as an individual person, things change. It becomes easy to see that your father or sister or brother-in-law is just an ordinary person doing the best they can to make sense of the world. And it becomes easier to see how they might make sense of it differently than we do, given their social-group identities and their experiences. Try asking yourself: How would I see the world if I was in this person's shoes, making sense of the world from their combination of identity groups? And how is my own social identity leading me to different paths of thought than theirs?

GO DEEPER THAN FACTS

Most of us believe that we see the world as it really is, so if we could just get the other side to see facts and reason, they would agree with us. Psychologists call this pervasive bias "naive realism," and it poses a powerful barrier to understanding one another. When others don't agree with us, we feel it must be because they are ignorant of the facts, too stupid to understand them, or too intellectually dishonest to admit they are wrong. So we try in vain to wrestle our opponents into submission with the sheer weight of facts and logic.

When researchers asked survey respondents what would make them respect their opponents' views, the most common answer was that if the views were based on facts and evidence, they would respect them more. Facts and evidence were mentioned more than twice as often as personal experiences. But the respondents' imagined answers turned out to be wrong. When psychologists Emily Kubin, Kurt Gray, and colleagues actually got people to discuss a contentious political topic with one another, facts and evidence did little to instill respect. Sharing a personal experience related to the issue, however, led partisans to respect their opponents much more. Citing statistics about gun deaths, for example, left people unmoved. But when a person shared how their support for gun control was shaped by a relative who was hit by a stray bullet, opponents of gun control had greater respect for their views, saw them as more rational, and were more willing to keep talking with them. The researchers found the same pattern for a range of controversial issues, from same-sex marriage to abortion.

One experience important to all partisan controversies is the experience of simply being heard. Psychologist Daniela Goya-Tocchetto and I found that people usually assume the worst about their opponents' motives. If a Republican says they want to cut taxes in order to grow the economy and help everyone, Democrats don't believe that the true motive is helping everyone. They think the Republican really just wants to make the rich get richer and hurt the poor out of spite. If a Democrat says they want to phase out fossil fuels to prevent global warming, Republicans believe that they are just trying to hurt coal miners out of pure malice.

At the bottom of these negative assumptions is a profound lack of trust. But we found that trust can be increased by making partisans feel that their voices have been heard. When policymakers talked to all sides before proposing the policy, participants trusted them more and were less harsh in their judgments about the true motives. Perhaps even more important, they were more willing to reach a compromise solution when they felt their perspective had been listened to. The interesting thing about these studies was that the policies were the exact same. It was only the experience of being listened to that changed.

We typically approach political conversations as debates to win or chances to persuade others to think the way we do. We think that if we just marshal enough evidence and display sound reasoning, we will change people's minds. But that approach ignores the power of the psychological immune system, which people deploy to keep their beliefs in place. They have developed their particular set of beliefs for the purpose of reassuring themselves that they are a good and reasonable person. So changing anyone's particular beliefs amounts to persuading them to admit that they are not as good or reasonable as they thought. People actively resist changing their beliefs, especially when someone is actively trying to challenge them.

The next time you are tempted to argue about politics, try setting aside the facts and issues that make up the surface-level argument. Ask yourself: What is going on beneath the surface level? Specifically, how is this person using ideas to defend their sense that they are a good and reasonable person? And even more important, how am I doing the same? Thinking about both participants in an argument as ordinary people trying to make sense of the world from where they stand helps in two ways. First, it combats the tendency toward dehumanizing, which we've previously discussed. And second, it allows us to really listen to one another. As soon as we start lecturing or arguing, we tune one another out. But listening and telling one another about our experiences and stories is a much more powerful way to understand one another.

This book is an extended exercise in understanding how people can see the world so differently than we do, without them being utterly alien to us. It is about how much common ground we really share as humans, despite how different we may seem. It is about how experiences, emotions, and rationalizations are more important in making sense of the world than cold, hard facts. And it is about how, behind even the most hostile opposing groups, there are individual people trying their best to fit into the world. I hope that anyone who understands those things will also understand by now that we ourselves are engaging in as much identity-based rationalization and self-protection as the people we disagree with.

So what do we do with this knowledge? Am I saying that both sides are equally right or justified in their vision of the future? Am I saying that we should just get along with one another no matter what the other side is doing to our country? No. The issues at stake are too important. They are worth fighting for.

The passionate urge to fight about politics is driven by a desire to make things better. But bringing about political change is separate from debating politics. Real political change happens with political work, not arguing on social media. Anyone can get involved with their local party precinct or activist groups and participate in grassroots political work. The local scale is where we can make the biggest difference. If we are willing to have fights with friends and family members but can't spare some time to stuff envelopes or knock on doors, how deep are our commitments? Precinct-level organizers, who are responsible for much of the real change happening, usually have little drama in their lives around politics. They are too busy doing the real work of political organizing to get into screaming matches.

Most Americans who are engaged in politics—and especially the highly educated ones—are what political scientist Eitan Hersh calls "political hobbyists." We may closely follow politics by reading newspapers obsessively and engaging on social media. But we engage in a way that is actually for our own entertainment or to express our own values rather than to make tangible changes in the world. This surface-level engagement makes us feel that we are contributing to the political process, but we are not actually changing anything. It is a kind of political sedative.

In Hersh's book *Politics Is for Power,* he details the ways that ordinary neighbors can organize entire neighborhoods for political action, and how any citizen can get involved at a local level. Making these kinds of changes requires a little advance planning and preparation in the form of deciding how you want to be involved. What are the priorities and issues you want to focus on? What kind of local action are you going to start getting involved in? Once you figure out how to get involved in a concrete way, the abstract ideas we argue about tend to fade into the background. If you are busy writing letters, making phone calls, or knocking on doors for a specific goal, it is easier to let the argument with your uncle slide.

Ultimately, I believe we have to learn to see each other two ways at once. The first view is as individuals doing our best to make sense of the world we are thrust into. It recognizes that we are all a product of our history and our circumstances. As Abraham Lincoln said of the southerners, "They are just what we would be in their situation." At the same time, we should view each other in a second way. We must see each other as opponents in a contest that matters. The point of remembering view number one is that it allows us to fight about view number two with words and ballots rather than blood and bullets.

Looking at people as products of their time and their circumstance provides a larger perspective, like looking at Earth from outer space. The distance helps us recognize that people are just people, muddling through their lives, making it up as they go along.

It doesn't make change any less urgent—quite the opposite. It reminds us that our children and grandchildren will likely view us as backward and morally blinkered. They will probably be right. But a better understanding of how we make sense of our circumstances, and they theirs, might help keep us connected anyway.

Acknowledgments

This book began as a daily rumination about where our country was headed, during the dark early days of the pandemic shutdown and the protests following the murder of George Floyd. I have many people to thank for turning my brooding and pacing into something you can hold in your hands. To begin, I thank Richard Pine, my agent, who helped shape the shards of an idea into a real book proposal. And Laura Tisdel and Rick Kot, my editors at Viking, who took a chance on that proposal and helped craft it into a complete book. Every page is better for their efforts. This book would not have been possible without my students, who have taught me so much, especially Heidi Vuletich, Jazmin Brown-Iannuzzi, Erin Cooley, Kristjen Lundberg, Daryl Cameron, Kent Lee, Jason Hannay, Manuel Galvan, and Neil Hester. The research behind the book was made so much better by my collaborators, especially Nicolas Sommet, Daniela Goya-Tocchetto, and Aaron Kay. I want to express my gratitude to two of my mentors, both of whom passed away in the last year. Sam McFarland, at Western Kentucky University, was always generous with his time and happy to give good advice when I stopped by his

ACKNOWLEDGMENTS

office with no appointment or warning. And Larry Jacoby, at Washington University in St. Louis, shared his brilliance and his insights with good humor. He never let a good theory go untested or a good story go untold. Finally, I thank my daughter, Lucy, who asks perfect questions and makes me realize how little I know.

Notes

Introduction

xiii an "ascent of man" type image: Martherus, J. L., Martinez, A. G., Piff, P. K., & Theodoridis, A. G. (2021), "Party Animals? Extreme Partisan Polarization and Dehumanization," *Political Behavior*, 43, 517–40.

xiii a strong predictor that political violence: Kelman, H. G. (1973), "Violence without Moral Restraint: Reflections on the Dehumanization of Victims and Victimizers," *Journal of Social Issues*, 29(4), 25–61; Leidner, B., Castano, E., Zaiser, E., & Giner-Sorolla, R. (2010), "Ingroup Glorification, Moral Disengagement, and Justice in the Context of Collective Violence," *Personality and Social Psychology Bulletin*, 36, 1115–29; Kteily, N., Bruneau, E., Waytz, A., & Cotterill, S. (2015), "The Ascent of Man: Theoretical and Empirical Evidence for Blatant Dehumanization," *Journal of Personality and Social Psychology*, 109(5), 901–31.

xiv the warning lights are flashing red: Kleinfeld, R. (2021), "The Rise of Political Violence in the United States," *Journal of Democracy*, 32(4), 160–76.

xiv one in three U.S. presidents: "Assassination Attempts on U.S. Presidents," WorldAtlas.com, https://www.worldatlas.com/articles/assassination-attempts-on-us-presidents.html.

xiv racial and religious divisions: Mason, L. (2018), *Uncivil Agreement: How Politics Became Our Identity*, University of Chicago Press.

xiv Racially motivated hate crimes: "Hate Crime Incidents," USAFacts.org, https://usafacts.org/data/topics/people-society/democracy-and-society/civil-rights/hate-crime-incidents/.

xiv 15 percent of Americans: Kalmoe, N. P., & Mason, L. (2022), *Radical American Partisanship: Mapping Violent Hostility, Its Causes, and the Consequences for Democracy*, University of Chicago Press.

xvi openness to experience: Furnham, A., & Fenton-O'Creevy, M. (2018), "Personality and Political Orientation," *Personality and Individual Differences*, 129, 88–91; Carney, D. R., Jost, J. T., Gosling, S. D., & Potter, J. (2008), "The Secret Lives of Liberals and Conservatives: Personality Profiles, Interaction Styles, and the Things They Leave Behind," *Political Psychology*, 29(6), 807–40.

xvii fear response to threats: Inbar, Y., Pizarro, D. A., & Bloom, P. (2009), "Conservatives Are More Easily Disgusted Than Liberals," *Cognition and Emotion*, 23(4), 714–25; Oxley, D. R. et al. (2008), "Political Attitudes Vary with Physiological Traits," *Science*, 321(5896), 1667–70; Hibbing, J. R., Smith, K. B., & Alford, J. R. (2014), "Differences in Negativity Bias Underlie Variations in Political Ideology," *Behavioral and Brain Sciences*, 37(3), 297–307. In addition to several studies finding a small correlation between political ideology and psychological responses to threats, some studies have failed to find any such association. These links between political ideology and threat responses should therefore be considered tentative: Bakker, B. N., Schumacher, G., Gothreau, C., & Arceneaux, K. (2020), "Conservatives and Liberals Have Similar Physiological Responses to Threats," *Nature Human Behaviour*, 4(6), 613–21.

xviii conservatives are cognitively rigid: Chirumbolo, A., Areni, A., & Sensales, G. (2004), "Need for Cognitive Closure and Politics: Voting, Political Attitudes and Attributional Style," *International Journal of Psychology*, 39(4), 245–53; Jost, J. T., Glaser, J., Kruglanski, A. W., & Sulloway, F. J. (2003), "Political Conservatism as Motivated Social Cognition," *Psychological Bulletin*, 129(3), 339–75.

xviii fundamentally different moral values: Graham, J. et al. (2013), "Moral Foundations Theory: The Pragmatic Validity of Moral Pluralism." In Devine, P., & Plant, A., eds. (2013), *Advances in Experimental Social Psychology*, 47, Academic Press, 55–130.

xix about 1 point more on a 6-point scale: Graham, J., Haidt, J., & Nosek, B. A. (2009), "Liberals and Conservatives Rely on Different Sets of Moral Foundations," *Journal of Personality and Social Psychology*, 96(5), 1029.

xix Essentialism is appealing: Gelman, S. A. (2004), "Psychological Essentialism in Children," *Trends in Cognitive Sciences*, 8(9), 404–9. For an extended discussion of psychological essentialism, see: Bloom, P. (2010), *How Pleasure Works: The New Science of Why We Like What We Like*, Random House.

xx 90 percent of Black Americans: Throughout the book, when citing data on political divides by race, education, religion, and urban versus rural voters, I rely primarily on reports from the Pew Research Center, as well as data from Gallup and voter file data from Catalist, including: Igielnik, R., Keeter, S., & Hartig, H. (2021), "Behind Biden's 2020 Victory: An Examination of the 2020 Electorate, Based on Validated Voters," Pew Research Center, https://www.pewresearch.org/politics/2021/06/30/behind-bidens

-2020-victory/; Ghitza, Y., & Robinson, J., "What Happened in 2020," Catalist, https://catalist.us/wh-national/#pp-toc-608eee40d2225-anchor-1.

Chapter One: The Roots of Our Division

10 "subduing her sister Southern states": For historical information about the Civil War and Reconstruction, I rely on a variety of sources, but especially work by historians David Blight and Eric Foner: Blight, D. W. (2001), *Race and Reunion: The Civil War in American Memory*, Harvard University Press; Foner, E. (2014), *Reconstruction: America's Unfinished Revolution, 1863–1877*, Harper Perennial Modern Classics.

11 before he escaped: For the biography of Josiah Henson, I relied on two main sources, Henson's autobiography and a biography of Henson by Jared Brock: Henson, J. (1852), *The Life of Josiah Henson, Formerly a Slave*, Charles Gilpin; Brock, J. A. (2018), *The Road to Dawn: Josiah Henson and the Story That Sparked the Civil War*, Hachette UK.

Chapter Two: Why You Can't Reason with Them

23 A few weeks after the 2020 election: For data on the results of the 2020 U.S. presidential election, see: Official 2020 Presidential General Election Results, Federal Election Commission, https://www.fec.gov/resources/cms-content/documents/2020presgeresults.pdf.

25 accused Joe Biden of sexual assault: Rutenberg, J., Saul, S., & Lerer, L. (May 31, 2020), "Tara Reade's Tumultuous Journey to the 2020 Campaign," *New York Times*.

27 how we predict our future feelings: Wilson, T. D., & Gilbert, D. T. (2003), "Affective Forecasting," *Advances in Experimental Social Psychology*, 35(35), 345–411; Gilbert, D. T., Pinel, E. C., Wilson, T. D., Blumberg, S. J., & Wheatley, T. P. (1998), "Immune Neglect: A Source of Durability Bias in Affective Forecasting," *Journal of Personality and Social Psychology*, 75(3), 617. For an in-depth exploration of affective forecasting and the psychological immune system, see: Gilbert, D. (2009), *Stumbling on Happiness*, Vintage Canada.

29 evaluate two welfare policies: Cohen, G. L. (2003), "Party over Policy: The Dominating Impact of Group Influence on Political Beliefs," *Journal of Personality and Social Psychology*, 85(5), 808.

29 symmetrical for Democrats and Republicans: Ditto, P. H. et al. (2019), "At Least Bias Is Bipartisan: A Meta-Analytic Comparison of Partisan Bias in Liberals and Conservatives," *Perspectives on Psychological Science*, 14(2), 273–91.

29 When researchers asked college students: Wirtz, D., Kruger, J., Scollon, C. N., & Diener, E. (2003), "What to Do on Spring Break? The Role of Predicted, On-Line, and Remembered Experience in Future Choice," *Psychological Science*, 14(5), 520–24.

31 they misremember their prior opinion: Markus, G. B. (1986), "Stability and Change in Political Attitudes: Observed, Recalled, and 'Explained,'" *Political Behavior*, 8, 21–44; Cameron, J. J., Wilson, A. E., & Ross, M. (2004), "Autobiographical Memory and Self-Assessment," *The Self and Memory*, 207–26; Rodriguez, D. N., & Strange, D. (2015), "False Memories for Dissonance Inducing Events," *Memory*, 23(2), 203–12.

31 the clinically depressed: Alloy, L. B., & Abramson, L. Y. (1979), "Judgment of Contingency in Depressed and Nondepressed Students: Sadder but Wiser?," *Journal of Experimental Psychology: General*, 108(4), 441; Lyubomirsky, S. (2001), "Why Are Some People Happier Than Others? The Role of Cognitive and Motivational Processes in Well-Being," *American Psychologist*, 56(3), 239; Mezulis, A. H., Abramson, L. Y., Hyde, J. S., & Hankin, B. L. (2004), "Is There a Universal Positivity Bias in Attributions? A Meta-Analytic Review of Individual, Developmental, and Cultural Differences in the Self-Serving Attributional Bias," *Psychological Bulletin*, 130(5), 711–47.

32 made people who they are: Strohminger, N., & Nichols, S. (2014), "The Essential Moral Self," *Cognition*, 131(1), 159–71; Strohminger, N., & Nichols, S. (2015), "Neurodegeneration and Identity," *Psychological Science*, 26(9), 1469–79.

33 rediscovered his true self: De Freitas, J., et al. (2018), "Consistent Belief in a Good True Self in Misanthropes and Three Interdependent Cultures," *Cognitive Science*, 42, 134–160; De Freitas, J., Cikara, M., Grossmann, I., & Schlegel, R. (2017), "Origins of the Belief in Good True Selves," *Trends in Cognitive Sciences*, 21(9), 634–36.

34 a Jewish family in Poland in 1919: For biographical information on Tajfel I rely on a biography by Rupert Brown, a former student of Tajfel's: Brown, R. (2020), *Henri Tajfel: Explorer of Identity and Difference*, Routledge. For a scholarly review of Social Identity Theory, see: Hogg, M. A. (2016), *Social Identity Theory*, Springer International Publishing, 3–17.

36 F-scale (for the fascist personality): Adorno, T. (2019), *The Authoritarian Personality*, Verso Books.

36 "the experiment requires that you continue": Milgram, S. (2009), *Obedience to Authority: An Experimental View*, Harper Perennial Classics.

37 coax people into going along: Asch, S. E. (1956), "Studies of Independence and Conformity: I. A Minority of One Against a Unanimous Majority," *Psychological Monographs: General and Applied*, 70(9), 1–70.

42 "cognitive response principle": Greenwald, A. G. (2014), "Cognitive Response Analysis: An Appraisal," in Petty, R., Ostrom, T. M., & Brock, T. C., eds. (2014), *Cognitive Responses in Persuasion*, Psychology Press, 127–33.

43 they think more, not less: Stangor, C., & McMillan, D. (1992), "Memory for

Expectancy-Congruent and Expectancy-Incongruent Information: A Review of the Social and Social Developmental Literatures," *Psychological Bulletin*, 3, 42–61; Hastie, R., & Kumar, P. A. (1979), "Person Memory: Personality Traits as Organizing Principles in Memory for Behaviors," *Journal of Personality and Social Psychology*, 37, 25–38; Petty, R. E., Tormala, Z. L., & Rucker, D. D. (2004), "Resisting Persuasion by Counterarguing: An Attitude Strength Perspective," in Jost, J. T., Banaji, M. R., & Prentice, D. A., eds. (2004), *Perspectivism in Social Psychology: The Yin and Yang of Scientific Progress*, American Psychological Association, 37–51.

43 **make an argument to explain their answer:** Trouche, E., Johansson, P., Hall, L., & Mercier, H. (2016), "The Selective Laziness of Reasoning," *Cognitive Science*, 40(8), 2122–36.

46 **the feeling of pain in general:** Lieberman, M. D., & Eisenberger, N. I. (2015), "The Dorsal Anterior Cingulate Cortex Is Selective for Pain: Results from Large-Scale Reverse Inference," *Proceedings of the National Academy of Sciences*, 112(49), 15250–55.

47 **good and reasonable to other people:** Mercier, H., & Sperber, D. (2011), "Why Do Humans Reason? Arguments for an Argumentative Theory," *Behavioral and Brain Sciences*, 34(2), 57–74; Mercier, H., & Sperber, D., eds. (2017), *The Enigma of Reason*, Harvard University Press.

Chapter Three: Ideology Without Ideas

54 **I read early conservative thinkers:** Fawcett, E. (2022), *Conservatism: The Fight for a Tradition*, Princeton University Press.

56 **Early liberal thinkers:** Priddat, B. (1990), *Traditions of Liberalism: Essays on John Locke, Adam Smith and John Stuart Mill*, Center for Independent Studies; Fenn, R. K. (1982), *Two Worlds of Liberalism: Religion and Politics in Hobbes, Locke, and Mill*, University of Chicago Press.

58 **"As government expands, liberty contracts":** Ronald Reagan, Farewell Address to the Nation, January 11, 1989, Ronald Reagan Presidential Foundation, https://www.reaganfoundation.org/ronald-reagan/reagan-quotes -speeches/farewell-address-to-the-nation-1/.

59 **"proud to say I'm a 'Liberal'":** Address of John F. Kennedy upon Accepting the Liberal Party Nomination for President, New York, NY, September 14, 1960, https://www.jfklibrary.org/archives/other-resources/john-f -kennedy-speeches/liberal-party-nomination-nyc-19600914.

60 **1936 presidential election:** Lusinchi, D. (2012), "'President' Landon and the 1936 *Literary Digest* Poll: Were Automobile and Telephone Owners to Blame?," *Social Science History*, 36(1), 23–54.

60 **political scientist Philip Converse:** Converse, P. E. (2006), "The Nature of Belief Systems in Mass Publics (1964)," *Critical Review*, 18(1–3), 1–74.

64 **put that idea to the test:** Kinder, D. R., & Kalmoe, N. P. (2017), *Neither Liberal nor Conservative: Ideological Innocence in the American Public*, University of Chicago Press.

65 **identify as Republicans:** Pew Research Center (2019), "Political Independents: Who They Are, What They Think," https://www.pewresearch .org/politics/2019/03/14/political-independents-who-they-are-what-they -think/.

67 **when their place in a hierarchy changes:** Brown-Iannuzzi, J. L., Lundberg, K. B., Kay, A. C., & Payne, B. K. (2015), "Subjective Status Shapes Political Preferences," *Psychological Science*, 26(1), 15–26; Brown-Iannuzzi, J. L., Lundberg, K. B., Kay, A. C., & Payne, B. K. (2021), "A Privileged Point of View: Effects of Subjective Socioeconomic Status on Naïve Realism and Political Division," *Personality and Social Psychology Bulletin*, 47(2), 241–56.

71 **a series of curious experiments:** Hall, L. et al. (2013), "How the Polls Can Be Both Spot On and Dead Wrong: Using Choice Blindness to Shift Political Attitudes and Voter Intentions," *PloS One*, 8(4), e60554; Hall, L., Johansson, P., & Strandberg, T. (2012), "Lifting the Veil of Morality: Choice Blindness and Attitude Reversals on a Self-Transforming Survey," *PloS One*, 7(9), e45457.

Chapter Four: Lincoln's Map

76 **"time of chalk":** For a general description of Earth during the Cretaceous period, see: Osterloff, E., "The Cretaceous Period: What Was Earth Like Before Dinosaurs Went Extinct?," Natural History Museum, https:// www.nhm.ac.uk/discover/the-cretaceous-period.html. For an accessible overview of the way Cretaceous chalk affected the spread of slavery and continues to affect modern politics, see: Dr. M (2012), "How Presidential Elections Are Impacted by a 100 Million Year Old Coastline," Deep Sea News, https://deepseanews.com/2012/06/how-presidential-elections-are -impacted-by-a-100-million-year-old-coastline/. For scholarly research on the links between the prevalence of slavery before the Civil War and modern-day racial attitudes and political behavior, see: Acharya, A., Blackwell, M., & Sen, M. (2018), *Deep Roots: How Slavery Still Shapes Southern Politics*, Princeton University Press; Payne, B. K., Vuletich, H. A., & Brown-Iannuzzi, J. L. (2019), "Historical Roots of Implicit Bias in Slavery," *Proceedings of the National Academy of Sciences*, 116, 11693–98.

77 **catastrophes that ever happened: chattel slavery:** For a detailed treatment of the history of cotton production and its role in the Industrial Revolution and the American Civil War, see: Beckert, S. (2015), *Empire of Cotton: A Global History*, Vintage.

79 **during colonial times:** For a history of justifications offered for slavery in the United States, see: Tise, L. E. (1990), *Proslavery: A History of the Defense of Slavery in America, 1701–1840*, University of Georgia Press.

81 a land dispute in 1765: DeVan, K. (2008), "Our Most Famous Border: The Mason-Dixon Line," Pennsylvania Center for the Book, https://pabook .libraries.psu.edu/literary-cultural-heritage-map-pa/feature-articles/our -most-famous-border-mason-dixon-line.

84 in each county that was enslaved: Hergesheimer, E. (1861), "Map Showing the Distribution of the Slave Population of the Southern States of the United States. Compiled from the Census of 1860." Washington, D.C.: Henry S. Graham, 1861, retrieved from the Library of Congress, https:// www.loc.gov/item/99447026/.

87 back to normal: Blight, D. W. (2001), *Race and Reunion: The Civil War in American Memory*, Harvard University Press.

88 three days later: Steers, E. (2014), *Lincoln's Assassination*, Southern Illinois University Press; White, R. C. (2009), *A. Lincoln: A Biography*, Random House; Stashower, D. (2013), "The Unsuccessful Plot to Kill Abraham Lincoln," *Smithsonian*, https://www.smithsonianmag.com/history /the-unsuccessful-plot-to-kill-abraham-lincoln-2013956/.

88 main goal for southern legislatures: For a comprehensive history of Reconstruction, see: Foner, E. (2014), *Reconstruction: America's Unfinished Revolution, 1863–1877*, Harper Perennial Modern Classics. For a shorter, accessible history of the struggle between North and South during Reconstruction, see: Foner, E. (2019), *The Second Founding: How the Civil War and Reconstruction Remade the Constitution*, W. W. Norton & Company.

94 Lynchings sometimes erupted spontaneously: *Lynching in America: Confronting the Legacy of Racial Terror* (2019), Equal Justice Initiative, https:// eji.org/wp-content/uploads/2019/10/lynching-in-america-3d-ed-080219 .pdf.

94 the fingerprint of slavery: O'Connell, H. A. (2012), "The Impact of Slavery on Racial Inequality in Poverty in the Contemporary US South," *Social Forces*, 90, 713–34; Reece, R. L. (2020), "Whitewashing Slavery: Legacy of Slavery and White Social Outcomes," *Social Problems*, 67(2), 304–23; Thompson-Miller, R., Feagin, J. R., & Picca, L. H. (2014), *Jim Crow's Legacy: The Lasting Impact of Segregation*, Rowman & Littlefield.

96 their parents' income, wealth, and education: For examples, see: Solon, G. (1992), "Intergenerational Income Mobility in the United States," *American Economic Review*, 82(3), 393–408; Bowles, S., & Gintis, H. (2002), "The Inheritance of Inequality," *Journal of Economic Perspectives*, 16(3), 3–30; Chetty, R., Hendren, N., Kline, P., & Saez, E. (2014), "Where Is the Land of Opportunity? The Geography of Intergenerational Mobility in the United States," *Quarterly Journal of Economics*, 129(4), 1553–1623.

96 tax data from Florence, Italy: Belloc, M., Drago, F., Fochesato, M., & Galbiati, R. (2023), "Multigenerational Transmission of Wealth: Florence 1403–1480," Centre for Economic Policy Research.

96 more powerful than individual talent: "Born to Win, Schooled to Lose: Why Equally Talented Students Don't Get Equal Chances to Be All They Can Be." (2019), Georgetown University Center on Education and the Workforce, https://cew.georgetown.edu/cew-reports/schooled2lose/.

97 top fifth of the income distribution: Reardon, S. F. (2011), "The Widening Academic Achievement Gap Between the Rich and the Poor: New Evidence and Possible Explanations," *Whither Opportunity*, 1(1), 91–116.

98 since the year 2000: Galvan, M. J. et al. (2022), "Is Discrimination Widespread or Concentrated? Evaluating the Distribution of Hiring and Housing Discrimination Against Black Americans," under peer review.

98 much more dramatic for wealth: Moss, E., McIntosh, K., Edelberg, W., Broady, K. (2020), "The Black-White Wealth Gap Left Black Households More Vulnerable," Brookings, https://www.brookings.edu/articles/the-black-white-wealth-gap-left-black-households-more-vulnerable/.

98 wealthy families spend five times as much: Reardon, "The Widening Academic Achievement Gap Between the Rich and the Poor: New Evidence and Possible Explanations."

100 negative attitudes toward Black people: Payne, Vuletich, & Brown-Iannuzzi, "Historical Roots of Implicit Bias in Slavery."

101 racial gaps in income and wealth: Sommet, N., & Payne, B. K., "Black Poverty Leads White Americans to Blame Racial Inequality on Black Americans Themselves," under peer review.

102 racial and political beliefs: Acharya, Blackwell, & Sen, *Deep Roots: How Slavery Still Shapes Southern Politics.*

103 to rate their feelings: Allport, G. W. (1954), *The Nature of Prejudice*, Addison-Wesley; Duckitt, J. (2005), "Personality and Prejudice," in Dovidio, J. F., Glick, P., & Rudman, L. A., eds. (2005), *On the Nature of Prejudice: Fifty Years After Allport*, Blackwell Publishing, 395–412.

104 Racial attitudes were a strong predictor: Goldstein, L. (2020), *Continuity or Change? Contextualizing the Role of Polarization and Racial Attitudes in the Trump Era*, University of California, Los Angeles.

104 views on the legitimacy of racial inequality: Mutz, D. C. (2018), "Status Threat, Not Economic Hardship, Explains the 2016 Presidential Vote," *Proceedings of the National Academy of Sciences*, 115(19), E4330-E4339; Abramowitz, A., & McCoy, J. (2019), "United States: Racial Resentment, Negative Partisanship, and Polarization in Trump's America," *Annals of the American Academy of Political and Social Science*, 681(1), 137–56; Riley, E., & Peterson, C. (2018), "Economic Anxiety or Racial Predispositions? Explaining White Support for Donald Trump in the 2016 Presidential

Election," *Journal of Race and Policy*, 14(1), 5–24; Sides, J., Tesler, M., & Vavreck, L. (2019), *Identity Crisis: The 2016 Presidential Campaign and the Battle for the Meaning of America*, Princeton University Press.

106 cash assistance to poor families: Brown-Iannuzzi, J. L., Dotsch, R., Cooley, E., & Payne, B. K. (2017), "The Relationship Between Mental Representations of Welfare Recipients and Attitudes Toward Welfare," *Psychological Science*, 28(1), 92–103.

106 the most common recipients of welfare benefits in the United States are White women: "Characteristics and Financial Circumstances of TANF Recipients, Fiscal Year 2010" (2012), U.S. Department of Health and Human Services, http://www.acf.hhs.gov/ofa/resource/character/fy2010/fy2010-chap10-ys-final.

106 voter identification laws: Brown-Iannuzzi, J. L., Cooley, E., Cipolli, W., & Payne, B. K. (2023), "Who Gets to Vote? Racialized Mental Images of Legitimate and Illegitimate Voters," *Social Psychological and Personality Science*, 14(3), 356–65.

Chapter Five: Goddamned Doctors and Lawyers

112 Accents tend to drift toward: Paquette-Smith, M., Buckler, H., White, K. S., Choi, J., & Johnson, E. K. (2019), "The Effect of Accent Exposure on Children's Sociolinguistic Evaluation of Peers," *Developmental Psychology*, 55(4), 809.

113 German sociologist Max Weber: Waters, T., & Waters, D. (2010), "The New Zeppelin University Translation of Weber's 'Class, Status, Party,'" *Journal of Classical Sociology*, 10(2), 153–58.

114 by a 55 to 44 percent margin: "Exit Polls" (2020), CNN, https://www.cnn.com/election/2020/exit-polls/president/national-results; Doherty, D., Gerber, A. S., & Green, D. P. (2006), "Personal Income and Attitudes Toward Redistribution: A Study of Lottery Winners," *Political Psychology*, 27(3), 441–58; Powdthavee, N., & Oswald, A. J. (2014), "Does Money Make People Right-Wing and Inegalitarian? A Longitudinal Study of Lottery Winners," IZA Discussion Paper No. 7934, http://dx.doi.org/10.2139/ssrn.2396429.

118 solving murders using a divining rod: Lynn, M. R. (2001),"Divining the Enlightenment: Public Opinion and Popular Science in Old Regime France," *Isis*, 92(1), 34–54.

120 makes people feel less control: Wegner, D. M., & Wheatley, T. (1999), "Apparent Mental Causation: Sources of the Experience of Will," *American Psychologist*, 54(7), 480.

126 not caused by education at all: This section on education and political

orientation relies on the following excellent papers, and each of these papers cites additional background research: Mariani, M. D., & Hewitt, G. J. (2008), "Indoctrination U.? Faculty Ideology and Changes in Student Political Orientation," *PS: Political Science & Politics*, 41(4), 773–83; Hanson, J. M., Weeden, D. D., Pascarella, E. T., & Blaich, C. (2012), "Do Liberal Arts Colleges Make Students More Liberal? Some Initial Evidence," *Higher Education*, 64, 355–69; Campbell, C., & Horowitz, J. (2016), "Does College Influence Sociopolitical Attitudes?," *Sociology of Education*, 89(1), 40–58; Strother, L., Piston, S., Golberstein, E., Gollust, S. E., & Eisenberg, D. (2021), "College Roommates Have a Modest but Significant Influence on Each Other's Political Ideology," *Proceedings of the National Academy of Sciences*, 118(2), e2015514117.

129 **why good events happen:** Olson, K. R., Banaji, M. R., Dweck, C. S., & Spelke, E. S. (2006), "Children's Biased Evaluations of Lucky Versus Unlucky People and Their Social Groups," *Psychological Science*, 17(10), 845–46; Olson, K. R., Dunham, Y., Dweck, C. S., Spelke, E. S., & Banaji, M. R. (2008), "Judgments of the Lucky Across Development and Culture," *Journal of Personality and Social Psychology*, 94(5), 757–76; Shutts, K., Brey, E. L., Dornbusch, L. A., Slywotzky, N., & Olson, K. R. (2016), "Children Use Wealth Cues to Evaluate Others," *PLoS One*, 11(3), e0149360; Elenbaas, L., Rizzo, M. T., & Killen, M. (2020), "A Developmental-Science Perspective on Social Inequality," *Current Directions in Psychological Science*, 29(6), 610–16.

130 **Non-White Americans favor Democrats:** CNN (2020), "Exit Polls."

130 **the less factual information people know:** Salter, P. S. (2021), "Learning History, Facing Reality: How Knowledge Increases Awareness of Systemic Racism," *American Educator*, 45(1), 26.

131 **When researchers cued people:** Sahdra, B., & Ross, M. (2007), "Group Identification and Historical Memory," *Personality and Social Psychology Bulletin*, 33(3), 384–95.

131 **continues to influence the present:** Rashawn, R., & Gibbons, A. (2021), "Why Are States Banning Critical Race Theory," Brookings, https://www.brookings.edu/articles/why-are-states-banning-critical-race-theory.

Chapter Six: Country People

138 **underestimate the risks:** Pierre, J. M. (2019), "The Psychology of Guns: Risk, Fear, and Motivated Reasoning," *Palgrave Communications*, 5(1).

138 **accidental shootings or homicides:** Kellermann, A. L., Somes, G., Rivara, F. P., Lee, R. K., & Banton, J. G. (1998), "Injuries and Deaths Due to Firearms in the Home," *Journal of Trauma and Acute Care Surgery*, 45(2), 263–67.

NOTES

138 the easier it is to get a gun: "Gun Safety Policies Save Lives" (2024), Everytown for Gun Safety, https://everytownresearch.org/rankings/.

138 right to have a gun: Parker, K., Menasce Horowitz, J., Igielnik, R., Baxter Oliphant, J., & Brown, A. (2017), "Guns and Daily Life: Identity, Experiences, Activities and Involvement," Pew Research Center, https://www.pewresearch.org/social-trends/2017/06/22/guns-and-daily-life-identity-experiences-activities-and-involvement.

138 "protection," followed by hunting: Pew Research Center (2023), "For Most U.S. Gun Owners, Protection Is the Main Reason They Own a Gun," https://www.pewresearch.org/politics/2023/08/16/for-most-u-s-gun-owners-protection-is-the-main-reason-they-own-a-gun.

139 a 30-point margin in 2016: Wasserman, D. (2020), "To Beat Trump, Democrats May Need to Break Out of the 'Whole Foods' Bubble," *New York Times*, https://www.nytimes.com/interactive/2020/02/27/upshot/democrats-may-need-to-break-out-of-the-whole-foods-bubble.html.

140 Places where trucks outnumbered cars: Gebru, T. et al. (2017), "Using Deep Learning and Google Street View to Estimate the Demographic Makeup of Neighborhoods Across the United States," *Proceedings of the National Academy of Sciences*, 114(50), 13108–13.

140 a map of nineteenth-century railroad connections: In this section I rely heavily on Jonathan Rodden's excellent book *Why Cities Lose*; Rodden, J. A. (2019), *Why Cities Lose: The Deep Roots of the Urban-Rural Political Divide*, Basic Books.

144 The Great Migration had begun: Tolnay, S. E. (2003), "The African American 'Great Migration' and Beyond," *Annual Review of Sociology*, 29(1), 209–32; Wilkerson, I. (2020), *The Warmth of Other Suns: The Epic Story of America's Great Migration*, Vintage Books.

146 the "social multiplier": Moretti, E. (2012), *The New Geography of Jobs*, Houghton Mifflin Harcourt.

147 compared the political leanings: Mummolo, J., & Nall, C. (2017), "Why Partisans Do Not Sort: The Constraints on Political Segregation," *Journal of Politics*, 79(1), 45–59.

148 their school years and afterward: Jokela, M. (2022), "Urban–Rural Residential Mobility Associated with Political Party Affiliation: The US National Longitudinal Surveys of Youth and Young Adults," *Social Psychological and Personality Science*, 13(1), 83–90.

149 "culture of honor": Nisbett, R. E. (2018), *Culture of Honor: The Psychology of Violence in the South*, Routledge.

150 historical records of baby names: Varnum, M. E., & Kitayama, S. (2011),

"What's in a Name? Popular Names Are Less Common on Frontiers," *Psychological Science*, 22(2), 176–83.

151 tested this idea in a famous experiment: Cohen, D., Nisbett, R. E., Bowdle, B. F., & Schwarz, N. (1996), "Insult, Aggression, and the Southern Culture of Honor: An 'Experimental Ethnography,'" *Journal of Personality and Social Psychology*, 70(5), 945.

153 the political leanings of people living there today: Bazzi, S., Fiszbein, M., & Gebresilasse, M. (2020), "Frontier Culture: The Roots and Persistence of 'Rugged Individualism' in the United States," *Econometrica*, 88(6), 2329–68.

Chapter Seven: God's People

158 only 55 percent of Democrats: In this section I rely on data from Robert Jones's *The End of White Christian America*: Jones, R. P. (2016), *The End of White Christian America*, Simon and Schuster.

159 between 80 and 85 percent of the world's population is religious: Pew Research Center (2012), "The Global Religious Landscape," https://www.pewresearch.org/religion/2012/12/18/global-religious-landscape-exec/.

160 suggests the real rate might be much higher: Gervais, W. M., & Najle, M. B. (2018), "How Many Atheists Are There?," *Social Psychological and Personality Science*, 9(1), 3–10.

165 sensitivity to ordinary agents: Barrett, J. L. (2009), "Cognitive Science, Religion, and Theology," in Schloss, R., & Murray, M. L. (2010), *The Believing Primate: Scientific, Philosophical, and Theological Reflections on the Origin of Religion*, Oxford University Press, 76–99.

167 leave behind the religion: Pew Research Center (2015), "Religious Switching and Intermarriage," America's Changing Religious Landscape," https://www.pewresearch.org/religion/2015/05/12/chapter-2-religious-switching-and-intermarriage/.

167 in strikingly regular ways: In this section I rely on data from Michele Margolis's excellent book *From Politics to the Pews*: Margolis, M. F. (2018), *From Politics to the Pews: How Partisanship and the Political Environment Shape Religious Identity*, University of Chicago Press.

169 linked to Republicans more than Democrats: Pew Research Center (2019), "Americans Have Positive Views About Religion's Role in Society, but Want It Out of Politics," https://www.pewresearch.org/religion/2019/11/15/americans-have-positive-views-about-religions-role-in-society-but-want-it-out-of-politics/.

170 trying to build a voting coalition: Balmer, R. (2021), *Bad Faith: Race and the Rise of the Religious Right*, William B. Eerdmans Publishing.

171 cast by White Christians: Jones, *The End of White Christian America*.

173 Søren Kierkegaard: Kierkegaard, S. (1843; 1985), *Fear and Trembling*, Penguin Books.

Chapter Eight: Unbelievable

179 the Rothschild family controls: Uscinski, J. et al. (2022), "Have Beliefs in Conspiracy Theories Increased over Time?," *PLoS One*, 17(7), e0270429.

180 related to conspiracy beliefs: Bowes, S. M., Costello, T. H., Ma, W., & Lilienfeld, S. O. (2021), "Looking Under the Tinfoil Hat: Clarifying the Personological and Psychopathological Correlates of Conspiracy Beliefs," *Journal of Personality*, 89(3), 422–36; Stasielowicz, L. (2022), "Who Believes in Conspiracy Theories? A Meta-Analysis on Personality Correlates," *Journal of Research in Personality*, 98, 104229.

181 "need for closure": Marchlewska, M., Cichocka, A., & Kossowska, M. (2018), "Addicted to Answers: Need for Cognitive Closure and the Endorsement of Conspiracy Beliefs," *European Journal of Social Psychology*, 48(2), 109–17.

183 5 percent of the variation in conspiracy beliefs: Yelbuz, B. E., Madan, E., & Alper, S. (2022), "Reflective Thinking Predicts Lower Conspiracy Beliefs: A Meta-Analysis," *Judgment and Decision Making*, 17(4), 720–44.

183 algorithms interact with human psychology: Enders, A. M. et al. (2021), "The Relationship Between Social Media Use and Beliefs in Conspiracy Theories and Misinformation," *Political Behavior*, 1–24.

183 What makes human users engage with a post: Van Bavel, J. J., Robertson, C. E., Del Rosario, K., Rasmussen, J., & Rathje, S. (2024), "Social Media and Morality," *Annual Review of Psychology*, 75, 311–40.

184 generally no higher today than it was in the 1970s: Uscinski, "Have Beliefs in Conspiracy Theories Increased over Time?"

186 who the villain is: Enders, A. et al. (2023), "Are Republicans and Conservatives More Likely to Believe Conspiracy Theories?," *Political Behavior*, 45(4), 2001–24.

188 Ivermectin and microchips: Motta, M., Hwang, J., & Stecula, D. (2023), "What Goes Down Must Come Up? Pandemic-Related Misinformation Search Behavior During an Unplanned Facebook Outage," *Health Communication*, 1–12.

189 calls a "rationalization market": Williams, D. (2023), "The Marketplace of Rationalizations," *Economics & Philosophy*, 39(1), 99–123.

190 vulnerable to being duped: Altay, S., & Acerbi, A. (2023), "People Believe Misinformation Is a Threat Because They Assume Others Are Gullible," *New Media & Society*.

191 Donald Trump's convention speech during the 2016 race: Nyhan, B.,

Porter, E., Reifler, J., & Wood, T. J. (2020), "Taking Fact-Checks Literally but Not Seriously? The Effects of Journalistic Fact-Checking on Factual Beliefs and Candidate Favorability," *Political Behavior*, 42, 939–60.

192 political advertising has almost no effect: Coppock, A., Hill, S. J., & Vavreck, L. (2020), "The Small Effects of Political Advertising Are Small Regardless of Context, Message, Sender, or Receiver: Evidence from 59 Real-Time Randomized Experiments," *Science Advances*, 6, 36.

193 he was being logically consistent: Miller, M. E. (2021), "The PizzaGate Gunman Is Out of Prison. Conspiracy Theories Are Out of Control," *Seattle Times*, https://www.seattletimes.com/nation-world/the-pizzagate -gunman-is-out-of-prison-conspiracy-theories-are-out-of-control/.

195 don't get too hung up on the details: Langdon, J. A., Helgason, B. A., Qiu, J., & Effron, D. A. (2024), "'It's Not Literally True, but You Get the Gist': How Nuanced Understandings of Truth Encourage People to Condone and Spread Misinformation," *Current Opinion in Psychology*, 57, 101788.

196 the impact of most kinds of corrections: O'Mahony, C., Brassil, M., Murphy, G., Linehan, C. (2023), "The Efficacy of Interventions in Reducing Belief in Conspiracy Theories: A Systematic Review," *PLoS One*, 18(4), e0280902; Lewandowsky, S. et al. (2020), *The Debunking Handbook* 2020, https://hdl.handle.net/2144/43031.

Chapter Nine: Winging It Together

201 estranged from a loved one: Homans, C., & McFadden, A. (2022), "Today's Politics Divide Parties, and Friends and Families, Too," *New York Times*, https://www.nytimes.com/2022/10/18/us/politics/political-division -friends-family.html; Pew Research Center (2019), "In a Politically Polarized Era, Sharp Divides in Both Partisan Coalitions," https://www.pewresearch .org/politics/2019/12/17/in-a-politically-polarized-era-sharp-divides -in-both-partisan-coalitions/.

201 increased by 400 percent in the last twenty years: Enten, H. (2021), "Statistically, Democrats and Republicans Hate Each Other More Than Ever," CNN, https://www.cnn.com/2021/11/20/politics/democrat-republican -hate-tribalism/index.html.

201 from 80 percent of the population to 60 percent: Jones, R. P. (2016), *The End of White Christian America*, Simon and Schuster.

203 false claims of voter fraud: Riccardi, N. (2022), "Support of False Election Claims Runs Deep in 2022 GOP Field," Associated Press, https://apnews .com/article/2022-midterm-elections-biden-cabinet-only-on-ap-election -2020-19131c0f468839bf2b847bd7b3dfaf5c.

203 Nineteen restrictive new laws: "Voting Laws Roundup: October 2021"

(2021), Brennan Center for Justice, https://www.brennancenter.org/our -work/research-reports/voting-laws-roundup-october-2021.

207 responded to a variety of political topics: Westfall, J., Van Boven, L., Chambers, J. R., & Judd, C. M. (2015), "Perceiving Political Polarization in the United States: Party Identity Strength and Attitude Extremity Exacerbate the Perceived Partisan Divide," *Perspectives on Psychological Science*, 10(2), 145–58.

207 when it comes to policies: Mason, L. (2018), *Uncivil Agreement: How Politics Became Our Identity*, University of Chicago Press.

208 disliked and dehumanized their own side: Moore-Berg, S. L., Ankori-Karlinsky, L. O., Hameiri, B., & Bruneau, E. (2020), "Exaggerated Meta-Perceptions Predict Intergroup Hostility between American Political Partisans," *Proceedings of the National Academy of Sciences*, 117(26), 14864–72.

209 viewing a collection of people as individuals: Cooley, E., Payne, B. K., Cipolli III, W., Cameron, C. D., Berger, A., & Gray, K. (2017), "The Paradox of Group Mind: 'People in a Group' Have More Mind Than 'a Group of People,'" *Journal of Experimental Psychology: General*, 146(5), 691.

211 Sharing a personal experience: Kubin, E., Puryear, C., Schein, C., & Gray, K. (2021), "Personal Experiences Bridge Moral and Political Divides Better Than Facts," *Proceedings of the National Academy of Sciences*, 118(6), e2008389118.

211 people usually assume the worst: Goya-Tocchetto, D., Kay, A. C., Vuletich, H., Vonasch, A., & Payne, B. K. (2022), "The Partisan Trade-Off Bias: When Political Polarization Meets Policy Trade-Offs," *Journal of Experimental Social Psychology*, 98, 104231.

213 Hersh calls "political hobbyists": Hersh, E. (2020), *Politics Is for Power: How to Move Beyond Political Hobbyism, Take Action, and Make Real Change*, Scribner.

Index